W9-AUU-413

Acknowledgments

A heartfelt "Thank you" is in order to the people who helped me pull this book together.

Thanks to the awesome team at Peachpit Press: Cliff Colby, who kept the boat on course; my poor bug-hating editor, Kathy Simpson; production editor Cory Borman, who re-created all the status-bar icons; compositor Myrna Vladic; and indexer Jack Lewis.

Sheldon Jones in the Verizon Wireless public relations department answered a litany of questions and loaned me the Droids I was looking for. Pam Boyd from Thomas/Boyd Communications was also great at answering questions and making sure that I had everything I needed to write this book.

I couldn't have written the book without background music. A special shout-out goes to Pandora One for providing the soundtrack, especially my Dub Reggae (Max Romeo, Augustus Pablo), Deep House (Silicone Soul, Paolo Mojo), and Lounge (Cantoma, Burnt Friedman) radio stations. If you want to check them out, visit www.pandora.com/people/info4596.

I'd be remiss if I didn't mention the Amtrak AutoTrain; Disney World; and Dad and Dot, not to mention their awesome oranges and pink grapefruit in Port Charlotte, Florida, where a lot of this book was written.

Most of all, a special thank-you to my wife, Liz, and my daughter, Ginger, who fed me and kept me motivated during my nocturnal hours; and to my parents, family members, and friends who supported me and understood when I disappeared during my long writing sessions.

Contents

About the Author

Jason D. O'Grady developed an affinity for Apple computers after using the original Lisa, and this affinity turned into a bona-fide obsession when he got the original 128 KB Macintosh in 1984.

He started writing one of the first Web sites about Apple (O'Grady's PowerPage; www.powerpage.org) in 1995 and is considered to be one of the fathers of blogging. He has been a frequent speaker at the Macworld Expo conference and a member of the conference faculty.

After winning a major legal battle with Apple in 2006, he set the precedent that independent journalists are entitled to the same protections under the First Amendment as members of the mainstream media.

O'Grady is also the author of *The Garmin nüvi Pocket Guide* and *The Google Phone Pocket Guide* (Peachpit Press), the author of *Corporations That Changed the World: Apple Inc.* (Greenwood Press), and a contributor to *The Mac Bible* (Peachpit Press). In addition, he has contributed to numerous Mac publications over the years.

When he's not writing about Apple for ZDNet at The Apple Core (http://blogs.zdnet.com/Apple), he enjoys podcasting and DJing.

For Liz and Ginger

The Droid Pocket Guide
Jason D. O'Grady

Peachpit Press
1249 Eighth Street
Berkeley, CA 94710
510/524-2178
510/524-2221 (fax)

Find us on the Web at: www.peachpit.com
To report errors, please send a note to errata@peachpit.com.

Peachpit Press is a division of Pearson Education.

Copyright © 2010 by Jason D. O'Grady

Executive editor: Clifford Colby
Editor: Kathy Simpson
Production editor: Cory Borman
Compositor: Myrna Vladic
Indexer: Jack Lewis
Cover design: Peachpit Press
Cover photography: Verizon Wireless
Interior design: Peachpit Press

ISBN-13   978-0-321-71193-9
ISBN-10   0-321-71193-9

9 8 7 6 5 4 3 2 1

Printed and bound in the United States of America

The Droid
PocketGuide

Jason D. **O'Grady**

Ginormous knowledge, pocket-sized.

**Peachpit
Press**

Say Hello to Droid

Before we get started, some housekeeping is order:

- *The Droid Pocket Guide* covers the Droid brand of mobile phones made by Motorola and HTC Corp., sold in the United States by Verizon Wireless. If you're using a Droid in another country or on another carrier, some screens and icons may look slightly different, but you should still be able to find your way around pretty easily with this *Pocket Guide*.

- The book covers two Droid handsets on the market as of February 2010: the Droid (Motorola) and the Droid Eris (HTC). I will refer to both handsets as *Droid* unless I specifically want to differentiate something that's specific to the Droid Eris.

- The Droid runs Android version 2.0, and the Droid Eris runs Android version 1.5. Because all Droids should be able to run Android 2.x by the time you read this book, I focus on Android 2.0 herein.

- Another cosmetic difference is that the Droid runs the stock version of Android, whereas the Droid Eris runs a customized Android user interface that HTC calls the *Sense* user interface, or Sense UI. This means that some icons and screens on the Droid Eris will be slightly different from those featured in this book, but don't panic; most of the functionality is the same on both Droid phones.

- If you're running a version of Android earlier than 2.0.1, some features covered in this book may not be available. I recommend that you upgrade your Droid's software to the latest version to take advantage of the newest features and bug fixes. You can upgrade by visiting the appropriate Web page:

  http://support.vzw.com/information/droid_upgrade.html

  http://support.vzw.com/information/droid_eris_upgrade.html

- Finally, it's important to note that because of Android's open-source foundation, any wireless carrier can modify the look and feel of Android to suit its needs. For this reason, some screens, icons, and behaviors may be slightly different from what you find in this book.

As you start down the path to mastering the Droid, having some background information will help you form a good foundation of knowledge to build on. In this chapter, I review some background on Google and Android, and discuss how the Droid came to be. Then I dive right into the phone itself, its features, what comes in the box, and some user-interface tips and tricks.

History and Background

One of the most compelling features of a Google phone is Google itself. The Silicon Valley search engine has grown into a search powerhouse that's used by just about everyone who uses the Internet. It's the default search engine in many Web browsers, which further contributes to its dominance. Google commands a substantial portion of search-engine market share in the United States—around 65 percent at this writing, which is more than quintuple that of its closest competitor (Yahoo).

It takes a trio of forces to get a mobile phone to market, with each one playing a different crucial role. Rounding out the trio are Google's manufacturing partners (Motorola and HTC) and its U.S. carrier partner (Verizon Wireless).

Let's take a look at the players.

Google

Google was started by Larry Page and Sergey Brin while they were students at Stanford University and was incorporated in 1998. Google's initial public offering in 2004 raised an eye-popping $1.7 billion, making the company's value closer to $23 billion. Google stock (ticker symbol GOOG) shot as high as $700 per share in 2007 but at this writing (January 2010) has settled at around $580 per share, making the company worth around $184 billion. Not bad for a couple of Stanford students.

The iconic Google home page is pictured in **Figure 1.1**.

Figure 1.1
The ubiquitous Google home page, now with an even skinnier design.

The name Google was derived from the word googol, which is 1 followed by 100 zeros, or 10^{100}.

The company delivered results for north of 300 million searches per day in 2009. Having conquered search, it has since branched out into providing online (also called *cloud*) applications such as Google Docs and Google Spreadsheets. Its free Web email service, Gmail, was introduced in 2004 and has grown to more than 150 million monthly users.

Most of these products are free, because Google subsidizes them with advertising, earning more than $23 billion in advertising revenue in 2009. Google's laserlike focus on specific keywords that *people are searching for* is highly desirable to advertisers and commands a premium price.

Google branched out into mobile search in 2000, delivering its fast, powerful search results to handheld devices such as smartphones. The company continues to refine and enhance its mobile-search product, and today, more than a third of Google searches in Japan are made on mobile devices.

Verizon Wireless

Verizon Wireless operates the largest wireless voice and 3G network in the United States, serving 89 million voice and data customers. Headquartered in Basking Ridge, N.J., Verizon Wireless is a joint venture of Verizon Communications (NYSE: VZ) and Vodafone (NYSE and LSE: VOD).

In addition to its impressive 89 million wireless phone customers, Verizon Communications, Inc., has 230,000 employees, 2,000 company-owned stores, and expected 2009 earnings of around $42 billion.

Verizon is certainly the big dog of all the carriers in the United States and is consistently rated highly in customer satisfaction surveys. It has the best network coverage where I live, but as they say, your mileage may vary.

Motorola and HTC

Two companies manufacture Droid handsets: Motorola and HTC.

The Droid (with keyboard) is manufactured by Motorola, a multinational, Fortune 100 telecommunications company based in Schaumburg, Ill. Motorola has been at the forefront of communications for more than 80 years and has many impressive firsts, including making the equipment that carried the first words from the moon and developing the first handheld cellular phone (the DynaTAC 8000x).

Motorola is best known for its StarTAC and RAZR mobile phones and is currently enjoying a resurgence in sales due to the popularity of the Droid.

The Droid Eris is manufactured by HTC, a Taiwanese firm founded in 1997. HTC quickly made a name for itself as the company behind many popular operator-branded mobile phones and launched its own line of phones under the HTC brand in 2006. HTC is one of the fastest-growing companies in the mobile-technology landscape, with revenue of $4.5 billion in 2009 and 8,100 employees worldwide.

Android

In 2005, Google acquired a company called Android, with the intention of creating a carrier- and manufacturer-independent mobile operating system that would run on almost any type of hardware. The Google Android (**Figure 1.2**) is the logo and mascot of the operating system by the same name and has become synonymous with mobile devices. I'd pick the Google Android over the Linux penguin in a fight *any* day.

Figure 1.2
The Google Android, the mascot and logo of the mobile operating system.

Consumers got their first chance to use Android on October 22, 2008, when T-Mobile released the G1 phone in the United States. The G1 is sometimes referred to as the *Google Phone*. (Did I mention that there's a *Pocket Guide* for it too?)

Android is an open-source operating system, meaning that it's free to use and modify under the Apache and General Public License (GPL) licenses, which makes it very appealing to developers. Everyone from mobile-phone carriers to handset manufacturers to individual developers can modify the operating system to accommodate specific needs. No costly licensing fees or restrictions are associated with Android, as there are with other operating systems.

note   **Droid is the hardware; Android is the software.**

Google is investing a lot of time and money in this operating system and is committed to making it a real competitor in the mobile-phone market. We're just starting to see the fruits of its labor. Developers are embracing Android because of its open-source roots and are signing up in droves to create applications (which I refer to as *apps* in this book) for the Android Market, which I cover in detail in Chapter 8.

After a slow start, Android is now available on more than 20 devices offered by 59 operators in 48 countries and 19 languages. HTC alone manufactures five Android handsets, and Motorola has shifted completely to the Android platform. Android market penetration is estimated to grow by an amazing 900 percent in 2009—easily outpacing the iPhone's predicted growth of 79 percent.

Android has already been adapted for use on tablet, netbook, and notebook computers, and it's so open that I wouldn't be surprised to see it running on your refrigerator door someday.

Open Handset Alliance

I'd be remiss if I didn't mention the Open Handset Alliance (**Figure 1.3**), a Google-led group established in 2007 to develop open standards for mobile devices. Its 50 member companies include most mobile-handset makers, application developers, carriers, and chipmakers.

Figure 1.3
The Open Handset Alliance logo.

OHA distributes the Android Software Development Kit (SDK) and source code on its Web site at www.openhandsetalliance.com.

If you ever wonder whether a particular phone carrier is going to release an Android phone, you can check OHA's list of member companies. If the carrier is on the list, there's a good chance that it's working on releasing an Android-powered device.

Features

There are several good reasons to purchase a Droid, including the fact that the feature set is always expanding. In fact, one of the biggest advantages of owning a smartphone—*any* smartphone—is that you can customize it infinitely by adding your own software. If you're a developer, you can create apps yourself; the rest of us have to download them from the Android Market (see Chapter 8).

To start this section, I look at core features that come with the Android operating system installed on the Droid.

Mobile phone

The primary reason for buying a Droid is the phone part. Right? Well, mostly yes, but it's probably not the main reason. Any way you look at it, the Droid and Droid Eris are very capable mobile phones.

The Droid (**Figure 1.4**) packs a whopping 3.7-inch capacitive touchscreen with haptic feedback and 854 x 480 (WVGA) resolution capable of DVD-quality playback. Also impressive is its 5-megapixel camera with autofocus, image stabilization, and dual-LED flash. The slide-out QWERTY keyboard, however, which may be an asset to many users, is flat, soft, and not much better than a virtual (onscreen) keyboard.

Figure 1.4
The Motorola Droid smartphone.

Courtesy of Verizon Wireless

Under the hood, Droid packs a Cortex A8 processor with hardware acceleration and CDMA 1X 800/1900 MHz, 3G EV-DO Rev. A (in the United States), 802.11b/g Wi-Fi, Bluetooth 2.1+EDR, USB 2.0 HS, and dual-microphone technology that improves call quality.

The Droid Eris (aka HTC Hero) is the less-expensive cousin of the Droid, featuring a smaller 3.2-inch display with 320 x 480 (qVGA) resolution. It also comes with CDMA 1X 800/1900 MHz, 3G EV-DO Rev. A (in the United States), 802.11b/g Wi-Fi, Bluetooth 2.0+EDR, multitouch capability, and a price tag that's about half that of the Droid.

tip You can check any U.S. address on the Verizon Wireless coverage map at www.verizonwireless.com/b2c/CoverageLocatorController. All the U.S. mobile carriers offer similar tools on their Web sites.

Email

Another important reason to buy a smartphone is to keep up with your ever-growing pile of unread email. The Droid allows you to stay on top of your mail in style.

The included email application seamlessly syncs messages from most POP3 (Post Office Protocol Version 3) and IMAP (Internet Message Access Protocol) services, and displays graphics and photos inline courtesy of its rich HTML viewer. Also, the QWERTY keyboard on the Droid is a huge asset when you have to compose a long message.

tip If you use Gmail exclusively, you're in luck! Android includes a dedicated Gmail application in its default installation. If not, don't worry. Android handles all IMAP, POP3, and Web-based email accounts without even breaking a sweat.

Gmail offers two-way synchronization of email in real time (also known as *push*), so you'll get notified when you receive new emails, even if you're in another application. Gmail even syncs draft emails, so you can begin writing a message on the Web and send it from the phone (and vice versa). Gmail for Android inherits many features from its desktop-based big brother, including labels, stars, and conversation view.

If you don't have the Gmail application on your phone, you can use the Web version (which is optimized for Android) at www.gmail.com or download it directly from the Market application. (See Chapter 8 for all the details on the Market.)

Messaging

Text and Multimedia Messaging Service (MMS) are extremely useful tools, and Android's Messaging application provides both in one app. Launch it to read and reply to messages you receive from your friends and colleagues. Received messages are threaded into a virtual conversation, making it easy to remember where you left off while bouncing among messages from different senders.

The Android Messaging application also makes it easy to flag, delete, and move groups of messages. The Droid's full QWERTY keyboard pays dividends for people who text a lot.

Web browsing

The Web browser included with Android combines Google's legendary search with a mobile version of its desktop Web browser, Chrome. Google chose WebKit for its Android browser. WebKit, an application framework that also powers Apple's Safari and Nokia's S60 browsers, is a full HTML Web browser with a zoom function that allows you to zoom in and out of any area of a Web page by touching small magnifying-glass icons at the bottom of the screen.

What's more, the Android Browser allows you to have multiple pages open concurrently, and its bookmark and history interface is similar to what you'd expect to find in a desktop Web browser. Simply press the Menu button to access these features. To illustrate the fact that Google thought of everything, the browser even includes *favicons*—the little graphics that appear before the URL and before the **<title>** tag in browser tabs.

Unfortunately, at this writing the Web browser bundled with Android doesn't support Adobe Flash technology. This means that if you visit a Web site that relies heavily on Flash (such as Hulu.com), you may not get the full experience. Some sites use Flash for site navigation, making it virtually impossible to find your way around if you're using a non-Flash browser.

Contacts

A phone isn't a phone if it doesn't have someone to call. Google has chosen an interesting method to sync contacts back and forth to the Droid: Google Contacts (www.google.com/contacts).

When you boot up your Droid for the first time, you'll be asked to log in to your Google account. After you log in, your contacts are synced automatically with the phone.

note If you're already a Gmail user, all your Gmail contacts will synchronize with your phone automatically. As you'd expect with a phone from Google, services from Google are baked into every aspect of the Android operating system.

The beauty of this system is that it's completely transparent and requires no user intervention whatsoever. You don't have to worry about USB cables, Bluetooth, or synchronization software; your contacts just sync in the background.

The down side is that if you're not a Google Contacts user, you'll have to import or enter your contacts to sync them to your phone. Fortunately, the process is Web-based (which definitely beats entering the contacts on the phone manually), and Google Contacts has excellent import tools.

The system supports importing contacts in the CSV (comma-separated values) file format from Microsoft Outlook, Outlook Express, Yahoo, and Hotmail.

tip You can sync directly from Apple's Address Book by choosing
Preferences > Accounts (*Figure 1.5*). If you want to perform a
one-time import from Address Book, use the freeware utility A to G
(www.macupdate.com/info.php/id/26427/a-to-g).

Figure 1.5
*The preferences
screen of Apple's
Address Book
application.*

Calendar

Just like contacts, the Droid's calendars sync with Google Calendar
(www.google.com/calendar). Whatever information is in your Google
Calendar gets synced with your phone automatically in real time, in
the background.

gCalendar (as I like to call it) is loaded with features, including sharing,
syncing with mobile phones and desktop software, reminders, invitations,
and offline mode—not to mention that it's completely free. You're all set.

As with Google Contacts, if you're already a Calendar user, you're all set up.
If you're not, you have a little work to do. Luckily, Calendar can easily import
event information in iCal or CSV (Outlook) format. To get your calendars
into Google, first export them from whatever software you're using now;
then follow the import steps on the Google Calendar Web site.

Google Maps Navigation

note Google Maps Navigation is available only for Android 2.0 on the Droid at this writing. It isn't available for earlier versions of Android (such as 1.5 and 1.6) that were originally included with the Droid Eris. According to HTC, the Eris will get upgraded to Android 2.0 in 2010.

One of the best Droid features is Google Maps Navigation, or just Google Maps, which provides turn-by-turn GPS navigation with voice guidance courtesy of its built-in GPS (Global Positioning System) chip. In fact, Google Maps is one of the key differentiating features of the Droid, because at this writing, it isn't available on any other mobile phone.

Google set the standard for Web-based mapping services on the desktop and has improved it even further for the Droid.

I can almost hear you asking, "How can mapping be better on a phone than on the desktop?" The simple answer is My Location, which uses your mobile phone's GPS chip to pinpoint your exact location. You don't have to enter your current location, because the Droid already knows where you are, which saves you a step. It gets even better when you add Droid's voice recognition to the mix. Instead of having to type the name of the store, post office, or bank that you're looking for, you can just speak the name, and Google Maps will convert it to text (with impressive accuracy) and perform the search for you.

But wait—there's more. Street View provides virtual street-level exploration from within the Maps app, courtesy of millions of pictures taken from a street-level perspective. The Droid's built-in magnetometer (digital compass) orients Street View according to your position and allows you to navigate 360 degrees simply by moving the phone around in your hand.

The Droid with Google Maps constitutes the best personal navigation device (PND) on the market right now, because it's always connected to the Internet. This connectivity gives Droid the competitive advantage of always having the latest maps; business information; and real-time data such as traffic and transit schedules. Currently, only 1 percent of PNDs are constantly Internet-connected.

Google Maps has the potential to replace an entire category of single-purpose GPS receivers and, therefore, is a truly disruptive technology. I cover this new and improved app in detail in Chapter 6.

YouTube

Google acquired YouTube in 2006 for $1.65 billion, and the child of this beautiful matrimonial union is a mobile YouTube application designed for the small screen and footprint of the Droid. Although YouTube is great for watching videos of dogs skateboarding, it's also the default video player for most applications on the phone. YouTube has lots of business applications too, but I can't think of any right now.

YouTube for Android is loaded with features, including a catalog of millions of keyword-searchable videos that you can browse (most popular, most viewed, top rated, most recent, and most discussed) and view in high quality. When you've found a video that you like, you can view its details and then favorite it, share it, rate it, and comment on it directly within the app.

In addition to viewing videos, you can upload videos to the popular video sharing site from both the YouTube and Camera apps. Also, you can log in to your YouTube account from the Droid and access your favorites, your playlists, and your own uploaded videos.

Search

Google is the undisputed king of search, so it's pretty natural to expect excellent search on Droid. You won't be disappointed. In addition to pedestrian tasks like searching the Web, images, blogs, news, books, and businesses, Droid allows you to search with your voice.

Voice search on the Droid is a powerful new feature that makes searching more convenient and safer than ever—especially while you're driving. It's available in the Web browser (where you'd expect it) and via the Quick Search box, which is a search widget for Android. The Quick Search box searches not only the Web, but also the content of your phone. You can scan apps, contacts, browser bookmarks, YouTube videos, music, and stock quotes, all directly from the search widget.

Because Droid is location-aware (thanks to GPS), searches are even more relevant, finding landmarks, retail stores, and services that are closest to you first. Although all this tracking and location-based stuff may sound a little Orwellian, GPS can be extremely powerful when it's put to good use. Besides, you don't have anything to hide, do you?

When you're performing more traditional searches (with a keyboard), Google Suggest helps speed your typing by making suggestions on the fly. Finally, because it's still Google at the end of the day, Droid search benefits from most of the features available in Google's full browser search. My favorite feature is relevance, which displays common search answers (such as weather, movie times, definitions, and sports scores) directly on the results page without requiring you to click another link. If you want to see the movie *Avatar*, for example, you can simply search for *Avatar* and your zip code, and you'll get theaters and movie times directly on the results page.

Unboxing

Now that I've whetted your appetite by describing all these juicy features, it's time for you to open the box and see what's inside. (Because you're reading this book, you've probably taken this step already, but just humor me, OK?)

note   This section of the book is based on the Droid distributed in the United States by Verizon Wireless. The Droid Eris and phones sold by other carriers will vary slightly.

What's included

The packaging of the Droid is quite nice, being compact and organized, but I don't want to spend too much time on it, given how fast these things change. (If my publisher paid me by the word, that'd be a completely different story, but it doesn't, so I'll move on.)

Inside in the package, you'll find the following items:

- Droid handset
- Rechargeable battery
- Mini USB wall charger
- USB-to-mini USB cable (for charging from a USB port)
- 16 GB microSD card
- Quick-start guide

A microSD card is preinstalled in the Droid, but the location leaves a lot to be desired. To access it, you need to slide off the rear panel (which comes off a little too easily for me) and remove the battery. Therefore, if you want to swap or install microSD cards, you'll have to shut down and reboot—a process that takes several minutes.

 Although 32 GB microSD cards have been announced, the largest card shipping as of February 2010 is 16 GB (about $40).

What's not included

Although everything that you need to get started is included in the box, you should consider purchasing a few extras:

- **3.5mm stereo headphones with microphone.** Remarkably, neither Droid model ships with microphone earbuds, meaning that you'll have to procure them on your own. Included buds are almost always terrible, though, so you're probably better off buying your own anyway.

  As with everything in life, you get what you pay for, and earbuds aren't any different. Expect to spend between $10 and $100, and make sure that they include a microphone for making phone and VoIP calls, voice searching, and recording voice memos.

- **Car charger.** Having a car charger is practically a requirement these days. If you like to keep your Droid's power-hungry radios and screen lit up all the time (and who doesn't?), your battery will drain faster than you can say "I'll call you back." Grab one for between $5 and $15, and make sure that it has the proper Micro USB plug on the end.

tip **If you plan to use your Droid with the excellent Car Mount for Droid from Motorola ($30), make sure that you buy a car charger with a cable long enough to reach the dashboard or windshield where you plan to mount it.**

- **Extra battery.** A second battery can be a lifesaver (literally) some times. Although the included 1300 mAh (milliampere-hour) battery is decent, if you like to use a lot of GPS, Wi-Fi, and Bluetooth between charges, you should probably buck up for an extra battery. Original-equipment batteries (Motorola model BP6X) cost about $35 online, and you can find aftermarket batteries for as little as $9.

> **tip** It's a good idea to check the charge of stored rechargeable batteries periodically. Dormant batteries lose approximately 10 percent of their charge per month.

- **A real case.** No case is included in the package, so you're on your own for this one. The fact that the Droid is a slider phone further complicates case options, relegating you mostly to sleeve-type models. That being said, it's better to keep your phone in a sock than nothing at all, because concrete and gadgets really don't match (unlike your socks). Just make sure that it's a clean sock.

  Literally hundreds of mobile-phone cases are on the market, and making a choice can be deeply personal. I'll leave you to your own devices to find one that suits your needs and personality.

- **Screen cover/film.** If you tend to be rough on your gadgets (as I am), it's a good idea to invest in a screen film. This clear film sticks onto the screen of the phone, protecting it from scratches from keys, coins, and anything else that might be in your purse or pocket. Prices range from $3 to $15, and it's money well spent (if you don't like scratches, that is).

Controls and User Interface

To fully realize the potential of your Droid, it's important to master the various hardware controls and interface elements that make all the magic happen. **Figure 1.6** gives you a close look at the controls and buttons on the Droid Eris oriented vertically (also called *portrait mode*).

Figure 1.6
The Droid, oriented vertically.

Courtesy of
Verizon Wireless

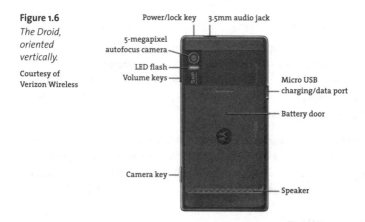

Power/lock key — 3.5mm audio jack

5-megapixel
autofocus camera

LED flash
Volume keys

Micro USB
charging/data port

Battery door

Camera key

Speaker

The Droid (not the Droid Eris, mind you) features a slide-out keyboard, shown in **Figure 1.7** in horizontal or *landscape mode*. Although the Droid is completely operable via its touchscreen with the keyboard concealed, many people prefer to use the hardware keyboard for texting and for composing email.

Figure 1.7
The Droid, oriented horizontally with its keyboard extended.

Courtesy of
Verizon Wireless

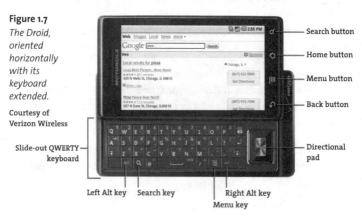

Search button

Home button

Menu button

Back button

Slide-out QWERTY
keyboard

Directional
pad

Left Alt key   Search key

Right Alt key
Menu key

Back button

Another unique feature of the Droid—and another one that's not available on the iPhone—is the Back button (refer to Figure 1.7). As you'd expect, it takes you back to the last screen that you viewed. In fact, the Back button operates exactly like the Back button in the Web browser that you've come to know and love.

The Back button also functions like the Escape (or Esc) key on a standard computer keyboard, in that it dismisses dialog boxes and the menu interface. If you want to get out of where you are but don't necessarily want to go home, the Back button is for you.

Menu button

The Menu button (refer to Figure 1.7) is extremely useful in Android, and it's not available on other popular phones, such as the iPhone. Pressing it displays a small overlay on the bottom portion of the screen, listing actions that are available in the current application. The Menu button is *contextual,* meaning that it presents different options depending on which app you're in. Usually, you can press it to find the various settings for a given application. (For more information on third-party applications, see Chapter 8.)

If you long-press the Menu button, the text labels below each option display their keyboard equivalents. Search becomes Menu+S, for example. People who use the keyboard a lot or simply are faster at typing sometimes prefer keyboard shortcuts to key presses.

Pressing the Menu button also unlocks the phone after the screen timeout interval (which you set by touching Settings > Sound & Display) has elapsed.

Home button

The Home button (refer to Figure 1.7) is equally intuitive. Pressing it takes you . . . well, home. It's a nice escape hatch from the depths of your Droid and a simple way to find your way back after an adventure through its various settings, menus, and applications.

tip Long-press the Home button to bring up a list of your most recently used applications. It's super-handy for switching between apps and functions, just like Command-Tab (Mac) or Alt+Tab (Windows).

Search button

Because search is a core feature of Android and the Droid phones, it's a perfectly logical choice for a hardware button. Pressing it brings up—you guessed it—the Quick Search box. Then you can type your search keyword or touch the microphone icon and begin speaking. For more information on the Quick Search box and voice search, see the "Search" section earlier in this chapter.

Keyboard (Droid only)

The hardware QWERTY keyboard on the Droid differentiates it from other Android phones, such as the Droid Eris. The vast majority of smartphone users probably would agree that a hardware keyboard is very desirable. Even casual emailers and pseudo-texters quickly realize the benefit of a hardware keyboard. Users who rely on their phones to send email and/or text messages regularly already know the value of a QWERTY keyboard and may even have purchased a Droid for this reason.

As keyboards go, the Droid's version isn't stellar. For one thing, I have trouble finding keys on it without looking. Also, although the Droid is a *phone* and isn't meant to replace a desktop computer's keyboard, I wish that the keys were a little taller, as they are on Palm smartphones. I also prefer keys that are a little rounder and more pebblelike—but hey, that's me.

tip If you'd like to have less bulk, or if you're fine with using a virtual (onscreen) keyboard, you're better off with the smaller and lighter Droid Eris.

Trackball (Eris only)

The trackball on the Droid Eris (**Figure 1.8**) is super-useful and an easy way to navigate the user interface. It's intuitive and requires little instruction, if any; simply roll it in the direction in which you want to move.

Figure 1.8
The Droid Eris offers trackball navigation.

Send key

End key

Trackball

Use the trackball to scroll around the home screen to choose an application, or use it as a controller in any of the many games that are available in Android Market. It also doubles as a button. After you've found the application that you're looking for, you can press the trackball to launch the application.

 In case you're wondering, this trackball is the same one that Research In Motion (RIM) uses on many of its BlackBerry devices.

Send and End keys (Eris only)

The Send and End/Power keys (refer to Figure 1.8) are going to be familiar to anyone who's ever used a mobile phone before. Press Send to place a call by dialing a number; press End to hang up a call, disconnecting the other party.

On the Droid Eris, the Send and End keys do a lot more. The Send key can also do the following things:

- Bring up the Voice Dialer (long-press)
- Open the recent call log
- Call a contact when a name or number is highlighted onscreen
- Add another call (while you're already on a call)
- Display the ongoing call onscreen (if you're in another application)
- Call the highlighted phone number (in the Browser, for example)

The End key hangs up an active phone call, as discussed at the start of this section, but it can also do the following:

- Lock the screen and put the phone in sleep mode
- Power off the phone (long-press)
- Toggle silent mode on or off

Now that you've had a look at the background, features, and general controls of the Droid, it's time to set up the phone up the first time and get acquainted with the status bar, notifications, and applications—all which you do in Chapter 2.

Alphabet Soup, Translated

Unfortunately, alphabet soup comes with the territory. All those three- and four-character acronyms are short for different cell phone technologies. If you aren't a technical junkie, here's what they all stand for:

- **CDMA:** Code Division Multiple Access

- **EV-DO:** Evolution Data Optimized

- **GSM:** Global System for Mobile communications

- **UMTS:** Universal Mobile Telecommunications System

2

Droid Basics

If you've already read Chapter 1, you saw that there's a lot going on under the Droid's hood and that it's packed with features. In this chapter, you dive headfirst into the basics of using an Android-powered phone—things that take a little time to master but soon become second nature.

This chapter builds on that strong foundation that you started in Chapter 1. I review the finer points of your Droid's battery and memory card, and give you an in-depth look at the home screen and application list.

Here we go!

Setting up Your Droid

On your maiden boot of a Droid, the phone steps you through several screens that are very important in the overall scheme of things. These screens help you set up your Google account, which will be the primary account on the phone. When you enter your Google account information, the Droid uses that information to sync your email, contacts, and calendar events from the cloud to your phone. (Flip back to Chapter 1 if you need a refresher on the cloud.)

After turning on the phone, you'll be greeted by the Android mascot. Then, if your phone is on the Verizon Wireless network in the United States, a message tells you that a special call needs to be placed to program your phone. During this call, you'll be prompted to press 1 to complete the programming.

After about a minute, you'll see another message stating that programming was successful and that it may take up to 15 minutes for service to start. (In my experience, however, the phone is activated almost immediately after the call.) When it does, you'll see a reassuring "Phone is activated!" message on the screen.

After touching Next, you'll get some helpful instructions on how to use your Droid. If you're using a Droid for the first time, take the time to step through the tutorials; they'll pay dividends in the future. If you're a Droid veteran or just impatient, you can skip the tutorials by touching the handy Skip button.

 You can return to the tutorial any time by touching Settings > About Phone > System Tutorial.

The next screen (**Figure 2.1**) prompts you to set up your Google account. Touch Next when you're ready to do just that.

Figure 2.1
*Time to set up
your Google
account.*

Several Ways to Say OK

In addition to touching the screen, you have several ways to
acknowledge the default button or selected option on the screen:

- On a Droid, you can press the Return button or the center of the
  directional pad on the keyboard.

- On a Droid Eris, you can press the trackball or the Send key on
  the bottom of the phone.

Some people find it quicker to press than to touch. As far as I'm
concerned, more choices for the user are always better than
fewer choices.

Setting up your Google account

The next screen (**Figure 2.2**, on the next page) asks you to create a new
Google account or sign in to your existing account.

Figure 2.2
*Sign in to your
Google account.*

Signing in is easy if you already have a Google account. Just touch the
Sign In button shown in Figure 2.2. Then, in the next screen (**Figure 2.3**),
enter your Google user name (or your Gmail address), followed by the
matching password, and touch the Sign In button in the bottom-right
corner. When you touch Sign In, you're agreeing to Google's terms and
privacy policies, which is required.

Figure 2.3
*Enter the user
name and
password
associated with
your Google
account.*

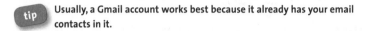

> **note** Any Google login will work here. If you've got a Gmail, Google Docs, or other Google password, you can use it to sign in. If you have more than one Google account, link your phone to the account you use most.

> **tip** Usually, a Gmail account works best because it already has your email contacts in it.

After you've promised your life away to Google, you're on your way to Google bliss! (Actually, it's not that exciting; I take it back.)

In the next screen (**Figure 2.4**), you're warned that it could take an entire *5 minutes* to set up your account. Time to mow the lawn! Don't be alarmed, though; my account took all of 90 seconds to set up over the Verizon Wireless network in my neighborhood.

Figure 2.4
After you enter your Google credentials, your Droid contacts Google to create your account.

Syncing your account

The next step—syncing your account information—is quick and painless. Initially, the phone doesn't download the thousands of emails, contacts, and calendar events you may have stored on the Google cloud—just your basic account info. After your account info is synced, your contacts, calendar events, and email download to your phone in the background.

When the syncing icon disappears from the status bar at the top of the screen (which I cover in more detail later in this chapter), the download is complete. Then you're off to the races and ready to start using your Droid right away.

note For more info on status-bar icons, see "Knowing Your Notifications" later in this chapter.

Getting online

Now that your phone is set up and accessing the Internet, it's time to put down the book for a while and have some fun. I encourage you to take 30 minutes to an hour to explore the phone's interface and applications. You'll get the hang of it really quickly. If you know how to use the Internet, you already know how to use the Droid.

On the home screen (**Figure 2.5**), touch the Browser application's icon to surf (press the Menu button for more options), or touch Phone to make a call. For a fun diversion, touch the gray arrow at the bottom of the screen to reveal a drawer containing all of the applications installed on your phone. I give you a detailed look at all these elements in "Touring the Home Screen" later in this chapter.

Figure 2.5
The Droid home screen.

Enjoy yourself—but come back to the book soon! I've got important things to say about batteries and expansion cards that you'll want to know about.

Charging and Conserving the Battery

The Droid comes with a rechargeable 1300 mAh (short for *milliampere-hour*) Lithium-ion battery that the manufacturer claims will allow you to talk for 6.4 hours or keep the phone on standby for 270 hours. Although the Droid's battery (shown installed in **Figure 2.6** and removed in **Figure 2.7**) is much better than that of previous Android phones, manufacturer battery specs are rarely achieved in real-world use. The good news is that with a moderate amount of conservation, you can expect to get a full day's use out of the included battery.

Figure 2.6
Rear view of the Droid with the battery and microSD card installed.

Figure 2.7
Rear view of the Droid with the battery and microSD card removed.

First charge

When you first start your Droid, the included battery can have anything from zero to a partial charge. Assuming that you don't have to run out the door *right now* with it or anything, I recommend connecting your phone to the wall charger to give it a good solid charge.

note The Droid is always on—and can't be turned off—when it's being charged. Luckily, you can still black the screen by pressing the power/lock key.

According to the manual, you should charge the Droid's battery fully before using the phone. Depending on how much charge remains, a recharge should take about 1.5 to 2 hours. I don't know about you, but there's almost *zero* chance that I'll put down a new gadget long enough to charge it fully. I recommend that you find a comfy chair next to an outlet, plug in the Droid, and explore a bit while it charges for the first time.

Like most Android-powered phones, the Droid comes with a Lithium-ion (abbreviated *Li-ion*) battery. This battery doesn't suffer from the "memory effect," in that you don't have to drain it completely before recharging it. I still try to fully charge my Droid's battery whenever possible, but this practice is mostly habit (and partly superstition?) and isn't necessary.

You have two ways to charge your Droid's battery:

- **Charger cable.** The charger cable came in the box with your phone. You've probably charged devices with a cable like this since you were 5 years old, so I'll let you figure that one out yourself. On the Droid, the Micro USB charging port is located on the top-left edge of the phone. (For more info on this port, see the nearby sidebar "Micro USB.")

- **USB port.** The alternative is to plug your phone into an available USB port on a computer, using the included USB cable (**Figure 2.8**). This method is a boon if you travel with a notebook computer, because you can charge your phone simply by connecting it to your notebook via USB.

Figure 2.8
Droid USB cable.

note To charge the Droid via USB, make sure that the host computer is awake—that is, not in sleep or hibernate mode. Most computers turn off their USB ports while they're sleeping, which would prevent your phone from charging.

note The maximum current draw for a standard USB port is about 500 mAh, whereas the current limit on the Motorola wall charger in the Droid box is 850 mAh. Translation: It will take longer to charge the Droid on a PC via the USB cable than it will if you plug the phone into a household AC outlet.

Charging schedule

Your charging schedule depends on how you use your Droid. If you're a casual user who places and receives fewer than ten calls per day and uses the phone's Internet features sparingly, I recommend that you charge your phone each night while you sleep. Although the phone may not *need* a charge at the end of each day, charging nightly is a hedge against the chance that you'll have an unexpectedly busy day tomorrow and your phone will run out of juice just when you need it most.

If you're a heavy user of features such as GPS and Wi-Fi, you can literally watch the battery meter trickle down as you use the phone, and you need to plan accordingly. Heavy users may have a tough time making it through a standard business day on a charged 1300 mAh battery, like the one included with the Droid. If this sounds like you, you'll want to read the upcoming sections on extra batteries and conservation methods.

Micro USB

The Micro USB port on the side of the Droid was developed by USB Implementers Forum, Inc. (USB-IF), an independent not-for-profit group that works to advance USB technology. Micro USB has become a standard for device chargers in Europe in 2010, and several companies—Motorola, Nokia, Sony Ericsson, LG, NEC, Qualcomm, RIM, Samsung, and Apple—have agreed to standardize on Micro USB for charging/connectivity technology in Europe.

Micro USB offers many advantages over the mini USB technology that it replaces. First is its smaller size, which is a requirement as mobile gadgets continue to shrink. Also, Micro USB is more durable than the mini USB connector. Micro USB plugs have a durable stainless-steel shell that is rated for more than 10,000 insertion cycles and a latching mechanism that provides higher extraction force.

Another benefit of the Micro USB specification is that it will support USB On-The-Go (OTG), a new technology that will allow portable devices to communicate directly without the assistance of a computer.

Battery life

Motorola claims that the Droid battery will allow you to talk for 6.4 hours or keep the phone in standby mode for 270 hours (11+ days). HTC estimates that the Droid Eris has 3.5 hours of talk time and 373 hours (15+ days) in standby mode when it's powered by a standard battery.

Unfortunately, these figures are perfect-world numbers that are used to market the phone and don't reflect typical use. (In the manufacturers' defense, however, battery life is extremely hard to quantify and benchmark, because everyone uses devices differently.)

Your Droid's battery consumption depends on several factors, most of which are common sense:

- **Phone activity.** Phone calls use battery power, so the more calls you make and take, the less time your battery will last.

- **Screen brightness and timeout settings.** It takes a lot of power to light up the large 3.7-inch screen on the Droid. Keeping the phone on longer than necessary, and keeping the screen brighter than necessary, will consume more battery power.

- **Radio use.** The *radios*—transmitters and receivers—in the Droid are major consumers of battery power, and the Droid has lots of radios. The Droid includes radios for CDMA (phone), 3G, Wi-Fi, Global Positioning System (GPS), and Bluetooth.

- **Camera use.** The Droid's 5-megapixel camera has as much horsepower as many point-and-shoot digital cameras, which is a drain on the battery. Taking pictures will reduce your battery life somewhat, but taking *videos* will reduce your battery even faster.

For tips on getting the most life out of your battery, read on.

Battery Conservation 101

High-tech smartphones with lots of power-hungry radios can chew through a charged battery pack before the clock strikes noon.

Implementing a couple of the following management and conservation techniques can make your battery go the extra mile:

- **Change your Power Control settings.** You can extend the Droid's battery life with the Power Control widget, which makes it easy to toggle such power-hungry settings as Wi-Fi, Bluetooth, GPS, data syncing, and screen brightness. Install it from the home screen by touching Menu > Add > Widgets > Power Control.

- **Turn off features that you don't use.** If you don't regularly use Wi-Fi, Bluetooth, or GPS, turn them off in Settings or via the Power Control widget (see the preceding item). If you don't need any connectivity, turn on airplane mode (touch Settings > Wireless & Networks).

- **Keep the screen at the lowest brightness that you can tolerate.** To adjust the brightness, touch Settings > Sound & Display, and scroll down to the bottom of the list. The same goes for the screen timeout setting: Keep it at 1 minute, and turn the screen off when you're not using it by pressing the End button.

- **Disable autosync if you don't need real-time email.** Touch Settings > Accounts & Sync; then clear the Background Data and Auto-Sync check boxes. Unchecking Background Data stops applications from syncing and sending/receiving data. Unchecking Auto-Sync stops the Droid from syncing data (email, calendar events, and contacts) automatically.

- **Use shortcuts for frequently used applications.** Using shortcuts (touch Settings > Applications > Quick Launch) saves screen taps and scrolls, and shortens the amount of time that the screen is on.

- **Install new firmware updates on your phone shortly after they're released.** Firmware updates almost always improve battery life in addition to adding features and fixing bugs. To check whether you're due for a system update, touch Settings > About Phone > Status > System Updates.

tip An application called Locale, which is available in the Android Market for $9.99, can manage almost every aspect of a Droid dynamically, including neat things such as automatically switching to your home Wi-Fi network when it's in range and turning off 3G and GPS. For details, see the Locale Web site (www.twofortyfouram.com). I cover third-party applications and the Android Market in Chapter 8.

Extra batteries

As I mention earlier in this chapter, smartphones eat through batteries faster than I get through turkey at Christmas dinner. Even a moderate Droid user will eventually need a backup battery. Luckily, replacement batteries (**Figure 2.9**) are relatively cheap—around $35 for an original Motorola pack and $15 for an aftermarket model—which makes purchasing one a no-brainer. Do yourself a favor: Pick one up, and keep it in your gear bag.

Figure 2.9
A replacement battery like this one comes in handy.

note Charge and rotate the batteries often. Batteries of this type lose about 10 percent of their charge per month and discharge completely before you know it.

If you want more power, you can purchase a battery as high as 2600 mAh for less than $50 on the aftermarket. This type of battery effectively doubles your Droid's run time. The problem is that physically larger batteries require a replacement rear cover to cover the extra bulge.

Think in terms of a trade-off: You can have longer run time if you're willing to add some size and weight in exchange.

note If you're a heavy user, you can purchase additional stock batteries or extended-life batteries (up to 2600 mAh) from sites such as www.seidioonline.com. Be wary, however, of high-capacity batteries that protrude from the rear of the phone, making your device larger and heavier.

Managing the Memory Card

A great feature of the Droid (and most other Android phones) is the included expansion-card slot, which allows you an infinite amount of expansion beyond the 256 MB that's available internally for app storage. Expansion cards have unlimited uses and capacity, and you can add as many cards as you need. The expansion-card slot is a key feature that's not available in the Droid's largest competitor: the iPhone.

The expansion-card slot on the Droid accepts microSDHC (Micro Secure Digital High Capacity) cards, which are even smaller than the SD cards used in many digital cameras. microSDHC (which I'll shorten to just *microSD*) memory cards are just a hair over half an inch on their longest side and are easy to lose, so keep them in a safe place.

The microSD card slot on the Droid is located on the bottom of the phone in the battery compartment (**Figure 2.10**). To access it, you must remove the battery door and—get this!—the battery. If it's not immediately evident why this requirement deserves an exclamation point, removing the battery shuts down the phone, which means that you need to shut down the phone to swap memory cards, and that's just plain dumb. Oh, well, at least the Droid *has* an expansion-card slot.

Figure 2.10
The microSD card slot is blocked by the battery.

note   Google refers to these cards simply as *SD cards* in some Android menus, but don't let that term throw you.

The Droid supports up to a 32 GB microSD card, but the 16 GB card that comes preinstalled should be more than adequate for most users. If you need additional storage, you can purchase more 16 GB cards for around $40 each.

Due to Moore's Law (which I define in the following tip) and the dynamics of book publishing, there's a good chance that 32 GB, 64 GB, or even 128 GB microSD cards could be available by the time you read this book. Before you buy such a card, make sure that the Android operating system you're running supports the larger card. A 32 GB card is a waste if your phone recognizes only 16 GB of it.

tip   Moore's Law describes a trend in the history of computing hardware in which the number of transistors on an integrated circuit doubles approximately every 2 years.

When a card is installed in the Droid, you can unmount it, format it, and view available storage by touching Settings > SD Card & Phone Storage (**Figure 2.11**, on the next page).

Figure 2.11
The SD Card &
Phone Storage
Settings screen.

Touring the Home Screen

Welcome home. I've been expecting you.

The Android home screen (**Figure 2.12**) is like your desk: It's where you use and organize your applications in a way that's most effective for you.

Figure 2.12
The Android
home screen.

Courtesy of
Verizon Wireless

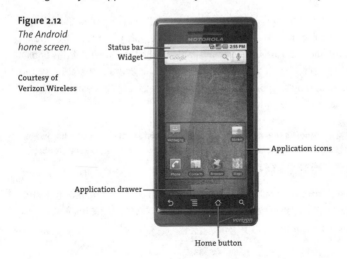

Status bar
Widget

Application icons

Application drawer

Home button

Because you go to the home screen after pressing the convenient Home button, you should dedicate it to shortcuts for your most frequently used applications. Out of the box, Google puts several of the most commonly used applications—Phone, Contacts, Browser, Maps, Messaging, and Market—on the home screen, along with one widget, which is that sleek Google search box across the top.

> **tip** You can swipe left and right on the home screen to reveal two additional home screens (for a total of three). These secondary home screens are great for storing shortcuts for apps that you use less frequently or that don't quite make the cut to the big leagues.

Customizing your home screen

The best feature of the home screen is that it's completely customizable. Touch and hold an icon, and a slight vibe tells you that now you can move that application. Touch and hold an empty space to add any application, shortcut, or widget to a home screen. My Android home screen is very dynamic, as I continually shuffle and shift apps between pages.

In addition to apps, the Droid's home screen can display *widgets*, which are little programs that actually run on the home screen. The Google search box at the top of Figure 2.12 is one example. In "Battery Conservation 101" earlier in this chapter, I talk about another useful widget called Power Control, which allows you to toggle various Droid settings; many other widgets display everything from clocks to the weather to your Twitter timeline.

Removing apps and widgets

When you want to remove an app or widget from the home screen (and this *will* happen), simply touch and hold its icon. You'll notice that the gray triangle on the application drawer turns into a trash can.

(I cover this drawer at the end of the chapter.) Simply drag the app to the trash can to remove it from your home screen. The icon and the trash can glow red when they touch, confirming the deletion (**Figure 2.13**).

Figure 2.13
To remove an app, simply drag it to the trash.

note This procedure doesn't delete the application itself from your phone—just the shortcut or alias to the app. For details on deleting the app, see the next section.

Uninstalling and managing apps

To permanently remove (or *uninstall,* in Android parlance) an application that you've downloaded, simply follow these steps:

1. Launch Android Market (see Chapter 8).

2. Press the Menu button.

3. Touch Downloads.

4. Scroll to the app that you want to uninstall.

5. Touch the Uninstall button.

You can also manage certain applications by touching Settings > Applications > Manage Applications to open the Application Info screen (**Figure 2.14**) and then touching the app's name. This method can be useful if you want to uninstall an app update that's causing problems or to manage the amount of space that an application is using. It also gives you a means to force-stop an app that's misbehaving.

Figure 2.14
The Application Info screen.

What's Your Status?

Another defining feature of Android is the ingenious status bar permanently affixed to the top of the screen (**Figure 2.15**). Think of the status bar as being a clearinghouse for all the alerts, messages, alarms, and other notifications you could possibly receive on a mobile device…and then some.

Figure 2.15
Android's status bar is one of its most useful features.

Touch the status bar to briefly display the date at the left end of the bar.

The Android status bar, like memory expansion and the removable battery, is another key feature that's not available on the iPhone. (I'm not trying to start any sort of class warfare or anything, but there are lots of benefits to having a Android-powered phone instead of an iPhone, and I'll continue to point out those benefits in this book.)

The status bar is rather small, so icons and symbols can be hard to discern, especially some of the less common ones. (I provide a chart of common notification icons in the following section.) You can pull down the status bar by touching it and dragging down without lifting your finger. This drag reveals a resizable (up to full-screen) display of all your current status notifications and more information about each one, such as your number of unread emails. Touching any of these extended notifications takes you directly to the application that produced it so that you can listen to the voice mail or read the text message, for example.

Equally handy is the large Clear button in the top-right corner of the screen (**Figure 2.16**), which removes many of the status notifications that can clutter the status bar. It's amazing how many notifications Android can generate, especially if you receive a lot of email and text messages—and if you're a user of social networks like Twitter, Facebook, and MySpace, be prepared to be inundated by notifications. The Clear button will come in handy plenty of times. (I cover notifications in detail in the next section.)

The status bar is available to every application that you download, so be prepared to see all kinds of new icons pop up in it from time to time. Luckily, almost every application allows you to choose how you receive its notifications. If your status bar is getting cluttered with alerts, like the one in **Figure 2.17**, press the Menu button when you're in the offending application; then find the setting to change the way that the app notifies you. Good applications offer many notification options; bad ones don't (and sometimes make it hard to find the notification settings).

Figure 2.16
Touching the Clear button declutters the status bar.

Figure 2.17
An example of status-bar overload.

Knowing Your Notifications

Notifications are integral parts of the Android ecosystem. They're used generously by the operating system and by most third-party applications too. Getting up to speed on the Droid's notification icons will make you much more efficient in using your phone, because you'll be able to iden-tify those icons at a glance.

Figure 2.18 shows a chart of the most common notification icons and their meanings. Most of these icons are self-explanatory; others, not so much.

@	New e-mail message		Ringer is off (silent mode)
	New text or picture message		Ringer on vibrate only
	Problem with text or picture message delivery		Phone is on mute
	New instant message		GPS is on and is working
oo	New voice mail		Uploading / downloading
1	Upcoming event		Content downloaded
	Alarm is set		GSM signal, roaming, no signal
	Song is playing		GPRS service connected, data flowing
	Data is syncing		EDGE service connected, data flowing
	SD card is full		3G service connected, data flowing
	More (undisplayed) notifications		Wi-Fi service connected, network available
	Call in progress		Battery charge indicators (full, half-full, low, very low)
	Missed call		Battery is charging
	Call on hold		Wireless services are off
	Call forwarding is on		Bluetooth is on, Bluetooth device connected
	Speakerphone is on		No SIM card

Figure 2.18
A table of the standard Android notification icons.

Working with the Application Drawer

The home screen (refer to "Touring the Home Screen" earlier in this chapter) is where you store frequently used apps, shortcuts, and widgets. Touching the application drawer (refer to Figure 2.12) opens the drawer to reveal a list of all the applications currently installed on your Droid (**Figure 2.19**).

Figure 2.19
An open application drawer, showing all your apps.

Applications are sorted alphabetically. You can scroll through them vertically by flicking upward or downward anywhere inside the open drawer. You can launch an app from the drawer by touching it, pressing the trackball (if you have a Droid Eris), or pressing the Return or Send key on the keyboard.

I discuss applications in much more detail in Chapter 8, which covers the Android Market. In the meantime, I want to dig a little deeper into the technology that makes the Droid tick—specifically, all those power-hungry radios that I mention in the battery section of this chapter. Turn the page to Chapter 3 to take a look at the Droid's hardware and chips.

3

Droid Hardware

In this chapter, I dig into a few of the Droid's key hardware features—specifically, its radios. *Radios* are the chips that the Droid uses for sending and receiving data via 3G, Wi-Fi, Global Positioning System (GPS), and Bluetooth. For the most part, these radios work invisibly, doing their thing silently in the background, but learning some subtle nuances of their interfaces can be helpful.

Although the topic can get a little technical, this chapter provides lots of information about the Droid's various radios, including the most important tip of all: how to turn them off to conserve battery life. I explore the features and benefits of four of the Droid's radios—3G, Wi-Fi, GPS, and Bluetooth—and show you how to maximize their performance.

If you don't particularly like to tinker with settings and configuration screens, this chapter may not be for you. Feel free to skip ahead to the chapters on fun aspects of the phone (such as software), if that's more your speed.

Wireless Acronyms

Although this information may be overkill for some readers, I think it's a good idea to start the chapter by giving you a quick overview of the various technical acronyms associated with the Droid.

Table 3.1 is a quick reminder of the acronyms used to represent wireless-network speeds and types of mobile data connections, and **Table 3.2** refreshes you on network acronyms.

Table 3.1 Speed Acronyms

ACRONYM	MEANING
Kbps Kilobits per second	1 thousand bits transferred over a 1-second period
Mbps Megabits per second	1 million bits transferred over a 1-second period
Gbps Gigabits per second	1 billion bits transferred over a 1-second period

Table 3.2 Network Acronyms

ACRONYM	MEANING
2G/2.5G (GPRS)	The 2.5G telecommunication hardware standard is a stepping stone between 2G and 3G that is capable of producing download speeds of 50–100 Kbps.

(continued)

Table 3.2 Network Acronyms (continued)

ACRONYM	MEANING
3G (third generation)	The third generation of telecommunication hardware standards is capable of generating data throughput of up to 14 Mbps (download) and 5.8 Mbps (upload).
4G (fourth generation)	The fourth generation of telecommunication hardware standards is capable of generating data throughput of up to 150 Mbps (down) and 30 Mbps (up) while moving and up to 1 Gbps while stationary.
CDMA2000 (Code Division Multiple Access)	This family of 3G mobile technology standards, based on CDMA, is used to send voice, data, and signaling data between mobile phones and cell sites.
GSM (Global System for Mobile communications)	GSM is a second-generation (2G) mobile phone system used by more than 3 billion people in more than 212 countries and territories; usually, it's voice-only.
Wi-Fi (wireless fidelity)	Wi-Fi usually is the fastest Internet access option, faster even than 3G. Speeds can vary widely, however, depending on the wireless access point you're connected to. I cover Wi-Fi in detail later in this chapter.
GPS (Global Positioning System)	GPS satellites help your phone calculate its longitude and latitude. Then the phone uses this information to pinpoint your location on a map. I review all kinds of other cool stuff that GPS does later in this chapter.

3G

Both Droid handsets are based on the third generation (3G) of telecom-munication hardware standards. 3G phones use advanced chips to communicate with transmitters on carrier radio towers to move data and voice packets back and forth more quickly and efficiently.

As you might expect, 3G phones are faster than *2G* phones, but you won't notice the difference immediately when making simple phone calls. The biggest advantage 3G has over 2G (or, more accurately, 2.5G) is in access-ing the Internet.

Apps that stream audio and video to your phone are the greatest benefi-ciaries of faster download speeds. 3G is capable of passing more data back and forth than 2G is, so the Internet feels much faster on a 3G phone. Sites load faster, and audio and video play smoothly.

3G devices are generally capable of downloading data at 14 Mbps and uploading at 5.8 Mbps—much faster than the lowly 2.5G standard that 3G replaces. The 2.5G standard can achieve download speeds of only 50 to 100 Kbps, so it can't handle audio or video streaming.

tip As I write this chapter in January 2010, carriers in some U.S. cities have started rolling out an even faster type of network called 4G (aka Long Term Evolution, or LTE). The 4G networks are theoretically capable of supporting downloads at 150 Mbps and uploads at 30 Mbps, with the potential to provide 1 Gbps Internet access to stationary users. Verizon Wireless expects to provide 4G coverage to most of the nation by 2012.

Coverage

Like anything that involves sending and receiving data, coverage can vary according to a variety of factors. Location, demand, structures, hardware, and software can all play a role in the signal quality that your device gets. Also, as you'd expect, 3G coverage can vary widely by city and carrier.

You can check your carrier's 3G coverage by going to its Web site and searching for a coverage map. For Verizon Wireless, you can find a coverage map at www.verizonwireless.com/b2c/CoverageLocatorController. For other carriers, Googling *coverage map* and the carrier's name should take you where you need to go.

Be forewarned, though: Don't take a coverage map at face value. Just because the coverage map *says* that your area is covered by a given network doesn't mean that it actually is. Because many variables can affect coverage, it's best to test the quality of the network *before* signing any long-term contract.

One easy way to do this is to borrow a friend's device that operates on the carrier in question. Vigorously test the quality of the voice and data network in the locations where you're going to use your device most—typically, at home and at work. Stress-test it by placing and receiving numerous calls and by streaming high-definition audio and video on the device at different times of day. Odds are pretty good that if the network is up to stuff on your friend's device, it'll work acceptably for you too.

Testing, however, isn't a guarantee. This type of test doesn't take into account changes in hardware and software if you're getting a different device from your friend's.

note   Another reason to test a network is the total cost of ownership of a Droid over a 2-year contract, which falls between $2,800 and $3,800. Considering the cost, it's critical to do your homework before signing on the dotted line.

If, after purchasing your Droid, you discover that your coverage isn't acceptable, don't fret. Verizon Wireless allows you to terminate service within 30 days of activation—for any reason. AT&T and Sprint offer similar return policies, but T-Mobile gives you only 14 days to change your mind.

Technology

Code Division Multiple Access (CDMA) is one of the two main competing network technologies for mobile phones in the United States. The other is Global System for Mobile communications (GSM). In this section, I cover both technologies.

note GSM networks continue to make inroads in the United States, and CDMA networks make progress in other parts of the world. Each camp firmly believes that its preferred architecture—GSM or CDMA—is superior to the other.

CDMA2000

CDMA2000, based on CDMA, is a mobile-technology standard that's popular in North America and parts of Asia; it's used to send voice and data between mobile phones and cell sites.

In 2009, 18 new CDMA2000 networks were added in rapidly growing markets (including China and India), pushing worldwide subscribers to more than half a billion people. More than 25 percent of those users are EV-DO mobile broadband users.

Major CDMA carriers in the United States include Sprint PCS, Verizon, and Virgin Mobile.

There are two types of CDMA2000:

- **1x.** Also known as 1x and 1xRTT (or *1 times Radio Transmission Technology*), 1x is the first and most basic CDMA2000 wireless standard. The standard supports packet data speeds of up to 153 Kbps, with real-world data averages between 60 Kbps and 100 Kbps.

- **1xEV-DO.** EVolution-Data Optimized (or just EV-DO) is a wireless telecommunications standard designed specifically for the transmission of data. Faster than straight 1x (above), EV-DO has a theoretical downstream rate of 2 Mbps and real-world download speeds between 300 Kbps and 700 Kbps, which is comparable to basic DSL.

  A faster version of EV-DO, called *Revision A* or just *Rev. A*, is capable of supporting data rates of 3.1 Mbps down and 1.8 Mbps up, although 1 Mbps down and 500 Kbps up are more realistic.

Actual download and upload speeds are based on a variety of factors, which I cover earlier in this chapter, so your mileage may vary.

GSM

Global System for Mobile communications (GSM) is a 2G mobile-phone system that's the primary competitor of CDMA. Like CDMA (which is used in the Droid), GSM sends voice and data between mobile phones and cell sites; unlike CDMA, it's used by more than 3 billion people in more than 212 countries and territories, outnumbering CDMA by a full 6 to 1.

Wi-Fi

There's no question that the Internet is a huge part of our lives, in part as a direct result of the proliferation of wireless access. In the not-too-distant past, accessing the Internet meant sitting down in front of a computer with a fixed network connection wired to a wall. Those wires went only so far, however, which meant that your surfing session expired as soon as you got up from the chair.

Well, no more. Since the invention of the wireless Internet router, you're no longer required to be tethered to an Ethernet or RJ11 cable plugged into the wall. You can use an inexpensive wireless router to surf the Internet from the couch, kitchen, or bedroom with ease. Now that wireless Internet access is everywhere (or so it seems), many gadgets come with wireless radios built in.

Android-powered phones are no exception. In fact, it's practically a requirement for a smartphone (does anyone else dislike that term?) to have wireless, or *Wi-Fi,* capabilities. In November 2008, Research In Motion (RIM) and Verizon Wireless released the BlackBerry Storm *without* Wi-Fi and were universally panned by critics (including me) for the omission.

Using Wi-Fi

Like most things on the Droid, Wi-Fi isn't very complicated to set up. Just touch Settings > Wireless Controls to access the Wireless & Network Settings screen (**Figure 3.1**), where you can set up everything you need to access a Wi-Fi network at your home or office. When Wi-Fi access is set up, your preferred wireless access points are stored on the Droid, so you can pretty much set it and forget it. Next time you're within range of a Wi-Fi access point that you've connected to before, the Droid will switch automatically from 3G to the faster Wi-Fi.

To connect to a Wi-Fi network, touch Settings > Wireless Controls > Wi-Fi Settings and then touch one of the listed networks in the Wi-Fi Networks section (**Figure 3.2**). Networks that are encrypted with a password (such as Frogpond in Figure 3.2) display a lock over the Wi-Fi icon and require you to enter a password to gain access. Open networks, which don't require a password, display the basic Wi-Fi icon sans lock.

Figure 3.1
*Wireless &
Network Settings
screen.*

Figure 3.2
*Wi-Fi Settings
screen.*

If you want to connect to a network that's not in the list, just touch Add
Wi-Fi Network at the bottom of the Wi-Fi Settings screen. In the resulting
screen (**Figure 3.3**, on the next page), enter the network's Service Set ID

(Network SSID), choose an option from the Security drop-down menu, and enter a password as appropriate for that particular network; then touch Save.

Figure 3.3
Adding a Wi-Fi network.

When you're connected to a Wi-Fi access point, you see an icon in the status bar. The four segments in the icon indicate how strong your connection is. A Wi-Fi icon with a question mark over it indicates a problem with the wireless connection.

Taking precautions

To wrap up this section, I want to leave you with a little anecdote about Wi-Fi security. In short, don't trust unknown networks with your confidential information. It's trivial to create a network called Starbucks, Marriott, or Hilton Honors and then monitor the traffic of anyone who connects to it—a practice called *spoofing*. A spoofed network is designed to look and operate like a normal Wi-Fi network, with one nefarious difference: The person who set it up could be scanning the traffic flowing through it for potentially valuable information.

If you plop down in a comfy chair in your favorite coffee shop and connect to the first free wireless access point that pops up, you could be connected to the laptop of the guy next to you, and he could be capturing your login information as you access your online bank account.

Not all free wireless access points are set up by hackers to steal your information, mind you. My point is that you must use common sense when using unknown Wi-Fi networks. Surfing the Web is pretty safe on a wireless network, for example, but logging in to your email account can expose your login credentials to a bad guy. I'd refrain from logging in to any financial Web site (bank, credit union, investments, and so on) whatsoever while you're logged in to a Wi-Fi network that you don't know. It's just not worth the risk.

tip   Change your passwords often, and use different passwords for different sites. Most people rarely change their passwords, and some use the same password for all the Web sites they access. Does this sound like you? You could be risking the security of your identity, because when bad guys have your password, they can do a lot of damage with it. A friendly warning: Don't be promiscuous in your wireless surfing habits.

GPS

One of the most useful features of the Droid is its dedicated GPS hardware, which gives you access to the 24 to 32 Global Positioning System satellites circling overhead. The GPS satellites provide the Droid hyperaccurate positioning data that previously was available only to the military.

GPS satellites broadcast signals from space, and GPS receivers like the one in the Droid use those signals to provide three-dimensional location (latitude, longitude, and altitude) and precise time. The heavy lifting is done on the handset itself, where apps like Google Maps (which I cover in

Chapter 6) translate the longitude and latitude coordinates sent by the satellites into a dot on a map representing your current location.

With an accuracy of 1 to 10 meters (depending on how many "birds" you're locked onto), there's no denying that GPS is perfectly suited for navigation. Its popularity is exploding as new smartphone apps designed for GPS flow into the market.

GPS-powered apps can display the exact distance to the pin on the golf course, tell you what restaurants and stores are in the immediate vicinity, and give you a weather report for your current location, all without asking you to enter your zip code—and these features are only the start. I list several innovative GPS apps in "Using GPS creatively" later in this chapter.

Using GPS

You can turn the GPS feature on and off easily with a quick trip to the handy Settings app. Simply navigate to Settings > Location & Security, and check (or uncheck) the green box next to Use GPS Satellites (**Figure 3.4**).

Figure 3.4
The setting to enable the GPS receiver is tucked away in the Location & Security Settings screen.

The Use Wireless Networks setting just above the GPS setting isn't what you think; it allows the Droid to determine your location via the wireless networks around you. Be warned, though: Checking this box means that you consent to sending anonymous location data to Google, even while no apps are running.

If you're not a heavy user, I recommend keeping GPS on all the time, because it adds a new dimension of utility to your phone (as you see in this section) with almost no down side. When this feature isn't in use, the GPS chip goes into low-power mode, saving precious milliamps. When you *are* using the Droid for real-time navigation, GPS use is a major battery hog; in fact, it's one of the biggest battery consumers on the Droid.

A little common sense goes a long way here. If you're planning an all-day walk, hike, bike ride, or any other event that will have you away from power for an extended period, you should turn off all unnecessary radios (like GPS) unless you need them. (See my battery-conservation tips later in this chapter.)

tip If you're a fan of automotive GPS receivers from Garmin, don't forget to pick up a copy of my *Garmin nüvi Pocket Guide*, also from Peachpit.

Using GPS creatively

If you think that GPS is useful in automotive applications, it's even more useful in a handheld device like a smartphone. The first and most common use of GPS technology is to get directions from point A to point B, which is an incredibly powerful feature. Tens of millions of people rely on GPS to get them to their destinations every day.

In a mobile device like the Droid, GPS is especially useful for getting directions for walking or using public transit (see Chapter 6).

You can use GPS technology in several other fun and creative ways, thanks to some third-party apps. Here's just a sample of the clever GPS-based apps available for the Droid:

- **Layar** (free) is a *reality browser,* which means that it uses an Android phone's camera, compass, and GPS position to add real-time information about your surroundings.

- **Wikitude** (free) is another reality browser that uses an Android phone's camera and compass to layer information over the live camera image.

- **Waze** (free) is a new service that promises to keep drivers informed about road conditions with real-time traffic updates.

- **Car Locator** ($2) helps you find your car in an airport or mall parking lot. This app is an Android Developer Challenge (ADC) winner.

- **My Tracks** (free) records the exact path of a run or bike ride and displays it as an overlay on a Google map.

- **Speed Proof** (free) allows you to use your phone as a speedometer.

- **GasBot** ($7 per year) finds the cheapest gas near your current location.

- **TeeDroid Caddy** (free) measures the distance to the pin from your current location on the golf course.

- **Orienteer** (free) is a fun app for *geocaching*—an outdoor treasure-hunting game that uses GPS devices.

- **Traffic Cams** (free) displays traffic and safety cameras near your location.

All these apps are available in the Android Market, which I cover in detail in Chapter 8.

One of my favorite GPS applications is FindMyPhone (99 cents), which helps you locate your Droid if you lose it or it gets stolen. If you have this application installed and misplace your phone, just send it an SMS text message (from another phone, obviously). Your lost phone will reply with its current location so that you can go recover it. The app can even make your Droid ring loudly for several minutes to help you find it when it's lost in your house. Brilliant! I need an app like this for my car keys.

Bluetooth

Bluetooth—an open wireless protocol for exchanging data over short distances—seems like it was invented for mobile phones. Compared with the 3G and Wi-Fi radios in the Droid, which are designed primarily for Internet access, Bluetooth has a short range. Bluetooth 2.1 with Enhanced Data Rate (EDR) supports theoretical data transfer speeds of up to 3 Mbps at a range of about 33 feet (10 meters), but you can expect more like 10 to 20 feet in the real world.

Bluetooth has many uses, such as creating personal area networks and sharing data between devices, but its primary application in mobile phones is wireless headsets. I cover the various applications of Bluetooth in the following sections.

Headsets

Although they make us look like Borgs wandering around talking to ourselves, Bluetooth headsets have become part of the technology landscape. There's no denying the convenience of being able to talk to someone on a mobile phone completely hands-free; it expands the freedom that started with cordless phones at home. The difference, of course, is that instead of being able to wander around our houses yapping, now we can walk just about anywhere in the world yapping.

Setting up a Bluetooth headset in Android is simple. After you initially *pair* (link) your headset and your Droid, the phone will remember the settings so that you don't have to repeat the pairing exercise each time you want to use your headset.

To get started, follow these steps:

1. Touch Settings > Wireless & Networks to display the Wireless Controls screen, which includes Bluetooth and Bluetooth Settings options (**Figure 3.5**).

   You can tell at a glance whether Bluetooth is turned on; if it is, you'll see a check in its check box.

Figure 3.5
The Wireless & Network Settings screen is where you change Bluetooth settings.

2. If Bluetooth isn't turned on, touch the check box to enable it.

3. Touch the Bluetooth Settings option to open the Bluetooth Settings screen (**Figure 3.6**).

   The Bluetooth Devices section of this screen is where all the action happens. Here, you'll see any Bluetooth devices that are within range of your phone and discoverable. If your headset isn't listed, make sure that it's in discoverable mode (if you're not sure how to do this, consult your headset's user manual for instructions) and then touch Menu > Scan for Devices.

Figure 3.6
The Bluetooth Settings screen is where you pair your Bluetooth devices.

4. When you see your headset in the Bluetooth Devices list (mine is called Jawbone in Figure 3.6), touch it.

5. If you're prompted for a personal identification number (PIN) for your headset, enter that code to gain access to your device.

   Consult your manual for your particular device's PIN, or search for it on Google.

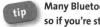 **Many Bluetooth headsets that I've used have a PIN of 0000 or 1234, so if you're stuck, those codes are good places to start.**

When Bluetooth is on, you'll see an icon in the status bar. The left icon in the margin here indicates that Bluetooth is on; the right icon indicates that you're connected to a Bluetooth device.

Like the other three radios covered in this chapter, Bluetooth drains the Droid's battery quickly when it's enabled, although not as quickly as GPS and Wi-Fi do. It's important to practice good conservation techniques and use Bluetooth sparingly when you're away from power for long stretches of time.

 Always use a wired or wireless headset when you use your phone while driving; in many states, it's the law.

Mind Your Mobile Manners

Although they have obvious safety benefits, such as allowing you to use a mobile phone while driving, Bluetooth headsets aren't a license to forget your manners and common courtesy. It's important to respect other people's personal space while you're in public. Too many people babble on their Bluetooth headsets (and mobile phones) at full register with no concern for the people around them.

Don't be that person! End your call when you're around other people (especially in confined spaces) or at least keep your voice down.

Bluetooth profiles

Bluetooth isn't limited to wireless headsets. It's also about *profiles*— wireless interface specifications for communication among Bluetooth devices. A total 28 Bluetooth profiles are available, each with a different application.

The Motorola Droid supports stereo Bluetooth 2.1 and the following profiles:

- **HSP (Headset Profile).** Allows Bluetooth headsets to be paired with mobile phones. Not surprisingly, this bad boy is the most popular profile of them all because it enables an entire category of wireless Bluetooth headsets to be used with your phone.

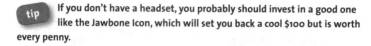

tip   If you don't have a headset, you probably should invest in a good one like the Jawbone Icon, which will set you back a cool $100 but is worth every penny.

- **HFP (Hands-Free Profile).** Allows a hands-free kit in a car to communicate with mobile phones inside the vehicle. More than 170 car manufacturers, from Audi to Volvo, now build in Bluetooth at the factory. This feature allows you to pair your phone with your car so that you can hear callers through your car's stereo system; callers hear you through a microphone installed near the driver's seat.

- **A2DP (Advanced Audio Distribution Profile).** Allows you to stream music from your Droid to a pair of wireless stereo headphones over Bluetooth—great for wireless headphones at the gym!

- **AVRCP (Audio/Video Remote Control Profile).** Provides a way to control TVs and other stereo equipment, turning the Droid into a universal remote control.

- **PBAP (Phone Book Access Profile).** Allows the exchange of Phone Book Objects between devices, typically used between the device and a Bluetooth car kit. This allows the Bluetooth in your car (see the HFP item earlier in this list) to access your contacts on your Droid so that you can look up and dial a contact's phone number from your car's touchscreen.

- **OPP (Object Push Profile).** Enables you to send pictures, business cards, and appointment details to another device. You could use OPP to exchange a contact or appointment between two mobile phones, for example, or between a mobile phone and a computer.

Power Consumption

The most important thing to keep in mind about the various radios in the Droid is that all of them draw power. There's a down side to slurping down all those delectable Internet bits at blazing speeds: shorter battery life. The more you use the radios in the Droid, the shorter your battery life will be. It's as simple as that.

This same principle goes for all the radios in the Droid: The more you use them, the more power they drain from your battery. Conservation rules the roost.

Conservation tips

For reasons that should be obvious, your phone's battery life can be a safety issue. You need to keep a close eye on your battery-management techniques to maximize battery life, especially while you're traveling. If you're going to be away from power for a long period—going hiking, camping, or rock climbing, for example—and need to rely on your phone for safety, it's imperative to turn off all unnecessary radios.

You should also disable the GPS, Wi-Fi, and Bluetooth radios in the Power Control widget (**Figure 3.7**) to conserve your battery for those critical times when you need it—such as calling for a ride home. I cover this handy widget in detail in Chapter 2.

Figure 3.7
The excellent Power Control widget.

Naturally, you can also save battery life by turning off all the various radios and screen brightness in the Settings app. Start by touching Settings > Sound & Display; then, in the resulting screen, set both Brightness and Screen Timeout (bottom of **Figure 3.8**) as low as possible. The minimum Screen Timeout setting, for example, is 15 seconds.

Figure 3.8

The Brightness and Screen Timeout settings are at the bottom of the Sound & Display Settings screen.

> **tip** If you're particularly worried about battery life, remember to turn off the screen by pressing the power or End button as soon as you finish using the phone. Don't wait for the screen timeout to kick in.

Conservation software

If you don't like having to dig through multiple layers of menus to find the Droid's radio settings, use the Power Control widget instead (refer to Figure 3.7 earlier in this chapter). This widget can extend the Droid's battery life by allowing you to toggle the power-hungry Wi-Fi, Bluetooth, GPS, data syncing, and screen brightness settings. Install it from the home screen by touching Menu > Add > Widgets > Power Control.

Another great application is Locale (**Figure 3.9**, on the next page), available for $9.99 from two forty four a.m. (www.twofortyfouram.com). Locale takes conservation up a notch by managing all your phone's settings dynamically, based on conditions such as location and time. With this app, you can specify a situation in which you never want your phone to ring—while you're in court, for example, based on what time you're in court or even where the court is located.

Figure 3.9
The Locale app allows you to change the Droid's settings dynamically.

Locale can change your phone settings based on your location data, which it gathers from your Droid's numerous radios. You can set a profile of settings for your phone to be enabled as soon as you come within range of your company's Wi-Fi network, for example, and another profile to be activated when you're on your home network.

You can also set up a Low Battery profile that turns off all but the essential Droid radios when battery power drops below a certain threshold—say, 20 percent.

Finally, if you're always missing calls when your phone is set to vibrate or mute mode, try Locale's VIP mode. It ensures that certain phone calls (such as those from the day-care center or your doctor) always ring through, even when your phone is in mute or silent mode.

That brings the hardware chapter to a close. Next, I want to give you a closer look at some of Android's core software applications—Phone, Contacts, and Calendar—which I do in Chapter 4.

4

Phone, Contacts, and Calendar

Whereas Chapters 1 through 3 were designed to give you some background and get you up and running quickly with your Droid, this section of the book is a little more hands-on. Now that you've got a solid foundation of knowledge, it's time to turn your attention to productivity—specifically, to the core applications on the Droid.

In this chapter, I focus on three applications: Phone, Contacts, and Calendar. These applications are absolutely essential to communications and productivity. I start with the basics and then show you a few tips that will improve your productivity and hone your skills.

Phone

Despite the emphasis on everything that smartphones can do, the phone is the most important component of these amazing devices. If your new smartphone doesn't work well as a phone—if it isn't reliable, and if it doesn't allow you to make an emergency phone call easily—it's basically useless and potentially hazardous.

The Droid has all the features that you'd expect in a modern mobile phone, and then some. As the Android operating system continues to evolve, it's only going to get better.

Phone app

The Droid's Phone application (**Figure 4.1**) is very sleek and simply designed, with four tabs across the top that give you easy access to all of its functions:

- **Phone.** This feature allows you to touch the screen to dial a number (although many people find it easier to tap the number on the keyboard).

- **Call Log.** The Call Log feature displays a list of your recent inbound and outbound calls. Pressing the Menu button gives you the option to clear the log.

- **Contacts.** Contacts contains all the names and phone numbers stored on your phone. I discuss this feature in more detail in the next major section of this chapter.

- **Favorites.** This features lets you store your frequently dialed numbers (family, friends, the office, and so on) in one convenient location. Touching the star icon on any contact's page adds that contact to your Favorites list.

Below the traditional 12-key dialpad is a row of three buttons: Voice Mail, Send, and Backspace.

Figure 4.1

The ubiquitous Android Phone application.

Voice Mail ——— Send ——— Backspace

Incoming and outgoing calls

Making a call on the Droid couldn't be much easier. Simply follow these steps:

1. Dial a number (including the area code, if it's not in yours).

2. Press the green Send button to initiate the phone call.

   While the phone is dialing, you see a series of call options (**Figure 4.2**):

Figure 4.2

During dialing, the Droid displays these call options.

- **Add Call,** which starts a conference call (see the upcoming "Conference Calls" section)

- **End,** which hangs up the call

- **Hide** or **Dialpad,** which conceal or bring back the dialpad (**Figure 4.3**)

Figure 4.3
Dialpad displayed during a call.

- **Bluetooth,** which enables a wireless headset
- **Mute,** which comes in handy for any number of reasons, including sparing the recipient of your call the shriek of a siren passing in the street
- **Speaker,** which places the call on speakerphone (see the next section)

3. Listen for the other party, and start talking when you hear him.

Because my daughter mastered this task at around age 1, I'm going to assume that you've got it covered.

When someone calls your Droid, his or her phone number is displayed on your screen. If the caller is in your contacts list, her name appears in addition to the number. To answer, press the green Send button.

As with most other mobile phones on the market, pressing the red End button—you guessed it—ends the phone call. No surprises there.

Speakerphone

To access the Droid's speakerphone feature, press the Menu button during any phone call to display the call-options screen (refer to Figure 4.2) and then touch Speaker. You'll hear your caller through the phone's larger speaker, and he'll hear you through the built-in microphone.

The speakerphone is excellent for long calls. It also comes in handy when someone's giving you instructions on how to upgrade your computer, for example, or when you need both hands free for delicate work or have to crawl under a desk.

note As handy as the speakerphone is, use it with discretion. Do *you* like being put on speakerphone? Most people don't, so ask for permission first. Also use it sparingly. Being underneath a car that you're trying to repair is a legitimate reason to put someone on speakerphone, but touching Speaker all the time because you're too lazy to hold the phone isn't.

Hang up and Drive

Using a speakerphone while driving is popular because it allows you to keep both hands on the wheel. Many U.S. states have passed laws making it illegal to operate a mobile phone while operating a motor vehicle, and speakerphones fall into a gray area. Driving while talking over a speakerphone technically is allowed in most states, but the phone has to be sitting on the seat or in a cup holder—*not* in your hand. As soon as you touch it to dial or hang up, you may be breaking the law.

I don't recommend using the speakerphone feature while driving because it's still a distraction. Instead, pick up a good Bluetooth headset (which I cover in Chapter 3).

Conference calls

Another powerful and somewhat underused feature of most mobile phones these days is the conference call. Conference calls are a super-handy way to shore up plans with multiple people, and they're dead simple to set up on the Droid, so there's really no excuse not to learn how to do it. Here's how:

1. When you have one person on the phone, press the Menu button to reveal the call-options screen (refer to Figure 4.2).

2. Touch Add Call, and dial the next party.

3. When the second party is on the line, press the Menu button again to reopen the call-options screen.

4. Touch Merge Calls (**Figure 4.4**).

Figure 4.4
Merge calls from this screen.

Congratulations—you've made your first conference call on the Droid. I told you that it's easy!

note There's no physical limit on the number of people you can have on a conference call on Android—just a practical limit. I think that managing more than five people on a call gets a little hard, but hey, that's me.

Call waiting

Just like your landline phone at home (if you still have one, that is), the Droid has call waiting built in. When you're on one phone call and another call comes in, you should see a screen that looks like **Figure 4.5**.

Figure 4.5
An incoming-call screen displays whatever details you saved for the contact, including a photo.

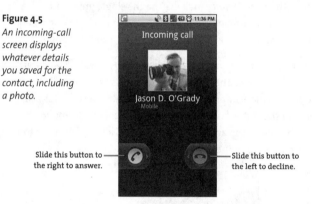

Slide this button to the right to answer.

Slide this button to the left to decline.

Most mobile carriers in the United States (including Verizon Wireless) include Caller ID in their plans, and Android displays the incoming phone number if it's not blocked or private. If the caller is in your contacts database, the Droid also displays that person's name and any image that you've attached to it (see "Editing contacts" later in this chapter).

If you don't want to interrupt your primary call, you can decline the incoming call by sliding the red button from the right side of the screen to the left side. When you do, the Droid transfers the call to voice mail. If you *do* want to take the incoming call, slide the green button from left to right. This action puts the current call on hold and answers the new one.

Voice mail

One consequence of the digital age is the proliferation of voice mail. Despite what the phone carriers tell you, however, it's unrealistic to expect to reach someone on her mobile phone any time, anywhere. As much as you may not want to believe it, people have families, jobs, and lives to deal with, and taking your phone call isn't always at the top of their list.

On one hand, voice mail can be frustrating. On the other hand, when it's combined with Caller ID, voice mail may be the single greatest privacy tool in the world. How many times has it saved you from taking a phone call at an inopportune time? You probably couldn't count them.

If you miss a call on your Droid, a little status-bar alert tells you about it. You can either pull down the status bar to reveal a larger notification with more information, as in **Figure 4.6** (see Chapter 2 for a refresher on the status bar), or you can get the same information by launching the Phone app and then touching the Call Log tab at the top of the screen (refer to Figure 4.1).

Figure 4.6
Missed-call information.

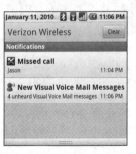

When you receive a voice-mail message, another status-bar alert pops up. As with missed calls, pulling down the status bar gives you more information about the message, including the Caller ID information and the time the call was received.

To retrieve a voice mail, just touch the status bar and slide it down; then touch the New Visual Voice Mail Messages alert. The key commands for saving and deleting voice mail vary from carrier to carrier, so I'm not going to cover them in this book.

Visual Voice Mail

Pioneered on the iPhone in 2007, Visual Voice Mail (VVM) came to Verizon Wireless in 2008 and is now available on the Droid. This new application lets you manage voice mail on the Droid through an easy-to-use screen (**Figure 4.7**) that provides one-touch access to your messages. At a glance, you can see who left a message and when.

Figure 4.7
The Visual Voice Mail application's main screen.

In addition, you can delete, reply to, and forward voice-mail messages without having to listen to earlier messages or voice instructions, so you can listen to important messages without first having to wade through messages that can afford to wait.

Verizon Wireless' VVM app has the following features:

- Onscreen access to message status

- One-button playback

- Temporary storage (40 messages for 40 days) and an option for permanent archiving

- Recording and playback of up to ten Caller ID-based greetings

- Reply via callback, text, or voice mail

tip Touching the voice-mail notification icon in the status bar is the fastest way to dial your voice mail.

note It's best to listen to the automated instructions all the way to the end when you first set up voice mail. This recording provides copious details on the carrier's voice-mail system, and it's good to take the time to learn all the options. Settle into a comfy chair and kick up your feet while you set up voice mail on your Droid. Soon, the commands will become familiar, and before too long, they'll be second nature.

Call forwarding

Call forwarding isn't nearly as sexy as some of the other features, but it's quite handy nonetheless. Suppose that you're taking a quick trip with your spouse, and you don't want to carry two phones. You can simply forward one phone's calls to the other. Call forwarding becomes essential when you've lost or misplaced a phone: Just forward your calls to another phone, and you're back in business (sort of). When your calls are forwarded, any new calls that come to the lost phone are forwarded to the other phone. Call forwarding can quickly become a necessity for people who lose their phones a lot.

Although call forwarding gets its own setting in the Call Settings screen on the T-Mobile G1, you won't find a specific setting for it on the Droid or Droid Eris. The Droid's Call Settings screen (**Figure 4.8**) allows you to enable automatic retry (handy for those mind-numbing repeat calls to Ticketmaster), TTY, hearing-aid compatibility, and enhanced voice privacy.

Figure 4.8
The Droid's Call Settings screen has lots of options, but call forwarding isn't one of them.

Because there isn't a call-forwarding option in Android 2.0.1 on the Droid (for whatever reason), you'll have to enable it the old-fashioned way: Dial *72 followed by the ten-digit number that you want to forward your phone to, and touch the green phone icon to dial. When you want to disable call forwarding, dial *73 and touch the dial icon.

The problem with this method is that you get no confirmation that call forwarding is set, and no indicator is displayed in the status bar to remind you that it's on.

tip If your Droid is lost or stolen, you can forward its calls to another phone by calling Verizon Wireless customer support at (800) 922-0204. If your account is set up for online access, you can also manage your call-forwarding settings at www.myverizon.com.

The good news is that Google is continually updating the Android operating system, and call forwarding has been spotted on other Android phones. With any luck, the Droid will get a dedicated call-forwarding option in a future release of Android.

Forward with Care

Keep in mind a few caveats before enabling call forwarding:

- The Droid must be powered up to forward calls. If its battery runs out, calls will no longer be forwarded.

- Airtime (minutes) applies to forwarded and transferred calls, even if you send the call to a landline (aka wireline) telephone.

- If you forward calls from your Droid to another mobile, *both* phones are using airtime.

- Don't forward calls to long-distance numbers if your plan doesn't include them. When you forward calls to numbers outside your local calling area, you're responsible for any toll, long-distance, and airtime charges incurred.

Contacts

Although I say earlier in this chapter that the phone is the Droid's most important feature, the Contacts application actually ties it for first place. Without your contacts, how would you remember a person's phone number, email address, or Twitter handle?

Contacts play a critical role on a mobile phone because they're your link to the outside world. They allow you to communicate with everyone who's important to you, which is a lot of people. Businesspeople would argue that contacts are everything because they're sources of revenue. If you're like me, you probably just want to be able to call home to find out what's for dinner and see whether you need anything from the store.

People seem to change phone numbers, email addresses, and street addresses more frequently than ever these days, though, so it's important to be vigilant about keeping your contact data current—if you want to actually reach anyone, that is. It's a never-ending task, which may be why Americans spend billions of dollars each year on contact management or customer relationship management (CRM) software.

If you have a Droid, however, you can save that money, because another of the Droid's many breakthrough features is its excellent data synchronization. Google has simplified the process tremendously by storing everything *on the cloud* (code for "on a Google server somewhere"), making it easier than ever to keep your ever-expanding contacts current. The process requires a little training and discipline, but storing your contact data on the cloud has two big benefits:

- You can access it anywhere that you can get an Internet connection.

- It's virtually impossible to lose your data (unlike your phone, which you have a 50 percent chance of losing).

Managing contacts on the phone

You have two main ways to manage contacts on the Droid:

 Launch the Phone app, and touch the Contacts tab.

 Launch the Contacts application in the home screen by touching its icon.

Either way, you see your list of contacts, which you can add to or edit as I describe in the following sections.

When you're viewing the Contacts list, pressing the Menu button brings up five options (**Figure 4.9**):

Figure 4.9
The Contacts tab has five options.

- **Search.** This option is pretty self-explanatory. Touch it to search your contacts. Although voice searching wasn't supported here as I wrote this chapter, I bet that it'll show up soon.

- **New Contact.** Touch this option on the Droid's touchscreen to add a new contact, and touch Done when you're finished. (I cover this process in detail later in the chapter.)

- **Display Options.** This option allows you to view only your contacts that have a phone number, which can greatly whittle down the list of contacts displayed on your Droid and make scrolling much faster. If you've got a bunch of contacts that have just email addresses, try activating this option.

- **Accounts.** The Accounts option lets you add contacts from a corporate, Facebook, or Google account. It also lets you enable or disable sync for each account, as well as toggle background data and autosync.

tip Limiting the number of contacts that you sync makes navigating your contacts faster and shortens sync time because less data is shuttling to and from the cloud.

■ **Import/Export.** As you'd expect, this handy option allows you to import and export contacts from an SD card. Contacts are exported in .vcf (vCard) format.

Adding contacts

To add a new contact, follow these steps:

1. Launch the Phone app.

2. Touch Contacts > Menu > New Contact.

   The Edit Contact screen opens (**Figure 4.10**).

Figure 4.10
Create a contact easily by entering some contact data and touching Done.

3. Fill in the appropriate details.

4. Optionally, you can scroll down to press the More button at the bottom of the screen (not visible in Figure 4.10) and enter even more data.

More data is always better than less, so if you have the time, enter as much contact data as possible.

5. Touch the Done button when you're finished.

tip On the Droid, the easiest way to add a new phone number is to dial that number (using the Phone app, naturally), press the Menu button, and then touch Add to Contacts before you press the Send button.

Contacts entered on the Droid are automagically synced to the Google cloud in the background—an amazingly useful and powerful feature.

Editing contacts

To edit or delete a contact, follow these steps:

1. Touch Phone > Contacts to display your list of contacts.

2. Search or use the scroll tab on the right side of the screen to find the contact you want.

3. Touch the contact's name to display its detail view (**Figure 4.11**).

Figure 4.11
A contact's detail view.

4. Press the Menu button; then touch the Edit Contact button to open the Edit Contact screen (**Figure 4.12**).

Figure 4.12
The Edit Contact screen for an existing contact.

5. Edit any of the fields for that contact.

6. Touch the Done button when you're finished.

7. If you want to delete a contact, just touch Menu > Delete Contact in any contact-editing screen.

If you want to get fancy, you can add photos of your contacts to their contact information by touching the framed-picture icon in the top-left corner of the Edit Contact screen (refer to Figure 4.12). Remember to touch Done when you're finished. Then, whenever you call a contact or a contact calls you, your Droid will display that person's picture. This feature is a nice personal touch but can take some time to set up, especially if you have a lot of contacts.

tip The contact screen for Amtrak AutoTrain (refer to Figure 4.11) is a great example of a clean, well-populated screen. Having complete contact data like this example makes interacting with your contacts infinitely easier and faster, and it's well worth your investment in time.

Your All-Star Contacts

Although you may have hundreds—or even thousands—of contacts stored on your phone, odds are that you probably call about a dozen of them 80 percent of the time. To make it easy to find the friends and family members whom you call all the time, make them favorites. Think of the process as creating bookmarks or shortcuts for those contacts.

To create a favorite, just touch the star in the top-right corner of that person's or company's contact screen (refer to Figure 4.11). This act places the contact in your favorites list so that it's easy to find on your Droid. Favorites appear in their own speed-dial section of sorts on the fourth tab of the Phone application (refer to Figure 4.1 earlier in this chapter).

You can star a contact in that person's Edit Contact screen on the Web as well as in the Droid interface. Just go to www.google.com/contacts; click a contact and then click the Edit button near the top of the screen.

Managing contacts with Google Contacts

Real-time, online data synchronization isn't a trivial task. Many companies have failed miserably at it by underestimating what's involved and how complicated it really is. Someone once summed up the situation by saying, "Sync is hard."

But not Google. The Droid synchronizes your data—automatically and in the background—with Google Contacts (www.google.com/contacts), Calendars (www.google.com/calendars), and Gmail (www.gmail.com).

Sync is a very powerful feature, and Google got it right with Android, providing it as a free service. How you use Google Contacts depends on whether you're starting from scratch or already using it. I discuss both approaches in the following sections.

Starting contacts from scratch

If you're new to Google, perhaps creating a new Google account just for your Droid, you should take a bit of time to set up your contacts. As I mention earlier in this chapter, contacts are integral to your phone, and having them organized and up to date is essential to having a good Droid experience.

Importing contacts

You can import any contacts in the CSV (comma-separated values) file format. The easiest way is to use the import tool in Google Contacts. Just follow these steps on your computer:

1. Log in to Google Contacts (www.google.com/contacts) from any Web browser.

2. Click the Import link in the top-right corner of the screen to open the My Contacts window (**Figure 4.13**).

Figure 4.13

Many people find it easier to add and import contacts on a desktop computer, using a real keyboard.

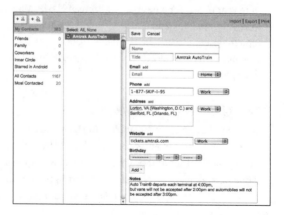

3. Click the Browse button, and select your contact file.

4. Click Import.

If you're using Windows, you can import data from Microsoft Outlook, Outlook Express, Yahoo! Mail, Hotmail, Eudora, and some other apps. Just export the contact data to a CSV file and then import that file into Google Contacts.

If you're using Address Book on a Mac, you have several ways to import contacts into Google:

- The simplest method is to choose Address Book > Preferences > Accounts, check the Synchronize with Google check box, and then click the Google button. You'll be prompted to log in with your Google account, and Address Book will sync in the background.

- A free utility for the Mac called A to G (www.macupdate.com/info. php/id/26427/a-to-g) exports a tidy CSV file to your desktop; this file imports easily into Google Contacts. The A to G utility is good for one-way migration to Google but doesn't offer syncing.

- An application called Spanning Sync (www.spanningsync.com; $25 for one year or $65 for a permanent license) allows Mac users to synchronize Address Book and iCal with Google Contacts and Calendars. The app may seem to be a little expensive, but it's worth the cost because it syncs bidirectionally (from Mac to Google, and vice versa) in the background.

Entering contacts manually

If you don't have a software application that Google Contacts can import contacts from, you can enter contacts directly by clicking the blue icon in the top-left corner of the Google Contacts window—the one showing one person next to a plus sign (refer to Figure 4.13 in the preceding section). Then just populate the fields, save your work, and move to the next contact.

tip You can add multiple phone numbers and email, street, and instant-messaging (IM) addresses by clicking the blue Add link next to each field name. You can also add custom fields for notes and other things by clicking More Information at the bottom of the window.

Already using Google Contacts

If you're already using Gmail or Google Contacts as your primary contact manager, you're way ahead of the game. Your contacts already live on the cloud and are ready to go; in fact, they've probably downloaded to your Droid already. Take a gander at the Contacts screen in the Phone app (refer to "Managing contacts on the phone" earlier in this chapter). If you see contacts that you didn't add manually, you're in business. How easy was that?

Troubleshooting contacts

If you're not seeing your Google Contacts entries on your Droid, here are a few things to check:

■ Did you sign in on your phone under the same account that you use for Google Contacts? Getting the account sign-on right is imperative. If you have more than one Google account, you may find it easy to mix up those accounts.

■ Are you in an area that has a solid data connection? Can you surf Web pages? If not, the problem is with your Internet connection.

■ If you set up your phone recently (as in hours ago), the contacts may not have fully synced from the cloud to your phone yet. Patience, Jedi, patience. Give it an hour or two.

After you've verified that your Google Contacts are synced between the cloud and your Droid, you're all set! Now you can call, email, IM, text (via Short Message Service [SMS]), or even map the address of any of your contacts directly from the phone—all of which I discuss in the next section.

Dialing, texting, emailing, and mapping a contact

Any time you're viewing contacts, you can communicate with that particular person or business in a couple of ways, right from the contact list:

- If you long-press a contact's photo, a little bar pops up, displaying quick contact options (**Figure 4.14**). Touch the appropriate option to call, email, text, or map that contact.

Figure 4.14
Long-pressing a contact's photo reveals the Quick Contact bar.

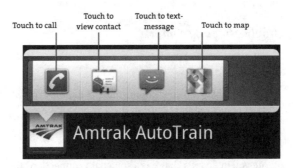

Touch to call   Touch to view contact   Touch to text-message   Touch to map

Amtrak AutoTrain

- To the right of each piece of data in the contact's detail screen (refer to Figure 4.11) is an icon representing the contact's phone number, email address, and so on. As you've probably guessed, touching that icon calls, messages, emails, or maps the contact that you're viewing. This feature is incredibly useful and centralizes all the ways to communicate with that contact.

Calendar

There's no question that the phone and Contacts features are integral parts of your mobile-phone experience. I close the chapter with the third biggie: Calendar.

Calendar is very feature-rich and frankly tough to beat, especially for the price. Google synchronizes its online calendars directly to Android phones over the air and completely free of charge. Many of the principles that I outline for Contacts earlier in this chapter apply to the Calendar application on the Droid; also, the two applications are linked in many ways. (If you jumped directly to this section, I recommend that you read the "Contacts" section before proceeding.)

The concept is simple: You can manage calendar events on the Droid itself or on the Web, depending on what suits you. Most people find it easier to enter and manage their calendars on a desktop computer because of the familiar keyboard and large screen. Droid syncing is bidirectional, so you can edit in either place, or both, and Google keeps both calendars in sync.

As with Google Contacts, the way you use Google Calendar depends on whether you're starting from scratch or already using it. I cover both methods in the next two sections.

Starting a calendar from scratch

If you're new to Google or have just created a new Google account for use with your Droid, you should take some time to set up your calendars. Like the phone and contacts, calendars are integral to the Droid experience, and having your mobile calendar organized will make you more productive.

Entering calendar events manually

The easiest way to enter calendar events is via the Web interface. Follow these steps on your computer:

1. Log in to Google Calendar (www.google.com/calendar) from any Web browser.

2. Click the Create Event link in the top-left corner of the screen (**Figure 4.15**).

3. Fill in the fields, and set the options.

   For details, see "Working with events and reminders" later in this chapter.

4. Click Save.

Figure 4.15
Events are easy to create in the Google Calendar Web interface.

Importing calendar events

If you already maintain a calendar in iCal or Microsoft Outlook, you can import it into Google Calendar with the handy online import tool

(www.google.com/calendar). The only catch is that event information must be in iCal or CSV (Outlook) format. If you're using a calendar
program that doesn't export to one of those formats, you need to export
the calendar data to a format that Google Calendar can read.

To import calendar data into Google Calendar from a desktop computer,
choose Add > Import Calendar; click the Add link in the Other Calendars
section in the bottom-left corner of the screen (**Figure 4.16**); and then
browse to the file that you exported from your previous calendar
application.

Figure 4.16
*The calendar-
import feature is
kind of hidden.*

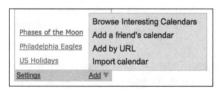

If you're new to Google Calendar, now would be a good time to famil-
iarize yourself with the full version on your desktop computer at your
own pace. The balance of this chapter focuses primarily on calendars
on the Droid.

Already using Google Calendar

If you're already using Google Calendar, pat yourself on the back, put
your feet up, and maybe even take an afternoon nap. Your calendar
events are already on the cloud and may already be synced to your Droid!

Launch the Calendar application on the Droid. If it looks like **Figure 4.17** (on
the next page), you're in business. Your calendar is already synced. If it's
blank, with no color bar on the right edge of each date, either you have
a light month planned or your calendar isn't synced (see "Troubleshooting
contacts" earlier in this chapter; those tips also apply to calendars).

Figure 4.17

The Calendar app on the Droid.

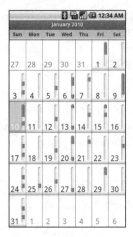

After you've verified that your Google Calendar data is synced between the cloud and your Droid, you're ready to roll. You can view your calendars, create events, and receive reminders.

Viewing a calendar

People most commonly use Google Calendar simply to view a calendar. About 90 percent of the calendaring I do on my phone is checking what's coming up today, this week, and this month. Usually, when a friend asks something like "Do you want to see Jay-Z on March 13"?, I'll whip out my phone, fire up Calendar, and zoom to that date.

tip Scroll between months by swiping your finger up and down the screen.

Pressing the Menu button while you're in the Calendar application (conveniently located in the application drawer) gives you options to view a day, week, or month at a time (**Figure 4.18**). Month view can get kind of cramped on the Droid's small screen, but luckily, touching a day switches you to day view, where you can read the details about events.

Figure 4.18
The Calendar in the 30-day view with menu options exposed.

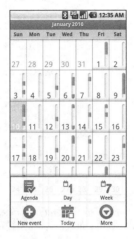

Using other calendars

Your calendar is very important because it allows you to make meetings and your kid's swimming lesson on time—but that's only the beginning. Google also allows you to create and maintain multiple calendars for things like clubs, groups, and sports leagues that you're involved in. One amazingly useful feature lets you view your significant other's calendar. Just have him or her set up a Google calendar and then click Add a Friend's Calendar in the Other Calendars section (refer to Figure 4.16 earlier in this chapter).

Also, you can sign up for an assortment of public calendars by choosing Add > Browse Interesting Calendars (**Figure 4.19**, on the next page). Calendars for everything from U.S. to international holidays and fun things like phases of the moon are accessible from the Google Calendar Web interface.

Figure 4.19
Some of the many free (and interesting!) Google calendars that are available.

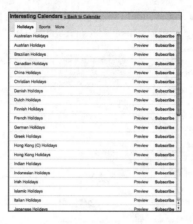

tip   I recommend setting up separate calendars for your work and personal events so that your vet appointments and sales meetings don't mix. Don't worry, though; you can still overlay all your calendars on one master calendar and view everything at the same time. Keeping separate calendars is best because it allows you to toggle the work calendar off while you're away on vacation and share only personal events with your family members (who couldn't care less about your next sales meeting, thankyouverymuch!).

You can control which calendars you see on the Droid by pressing the Menu button and then touching More > My Calendars (**Figure 4.20**). My Calendars allows you to toggle the display of calendars on and off by checking and clearing check boxes to the left of those calendars' names. A green check means that the calendar is being displayed on your phone; a gray check means that it *isn't* being displayed (as weird as that sounds).

You can add and delete calendars by pressing the Menu button while you're in the My Calendars screen. You'll see two buttons at the bottom of the screen for—what else?—adding and removing calendars. Didn't I tell you that this was going to be easy?

Figure 4.20
My Calendars allows you to select which calendars you which to view.

Working with events and reminders

When a friend asks whether you're available on a certain day, and you discover that you are by checking your calendar, it's best to create a new event right there on the spot. Sure, it's easy to say that you'll remember the event and put it in your calendar later, but if you're like me, doing that is virtually impossible. If I don't enter an event in my calendar right away, it usually doesn't happen. Taking time to create a new event *the minute that it's confirmed* will pay off down the road.

You have two primary ways to create events (or appointments, or meetings) on the Droid:

- Touch Calendar > Menu > New Event.
- Long-press a specific day and time in any of the calendar views (day, week, or month).

Either method brings up the Event Details screen (**Figure 4.21**, on the next page). Just complete a few of the whos and whats about the event, and press the Save button. The new event immediately appears on your Droid's calendar and synchronizes with the desktop version of Google Calendar within a few minutes.

Figure 4.21

The Event Details screen allows you to view and edit details.

Reminders are important aspects of the whole event-creation process and therefore worth reviewing. When you add a new event, by default the phone is set to give you a lowly 10-minute reminder, which isn't enough time to make it to the dry cleaner's down the street, let alone to catch a flight. You can set reminders any time you create or edit a calendar event (on the phone or on the Web) as far as a week out, but I usually choose a 2-hour reminder for local events, which allows me enough time for preparation and travel.

Reminder icons appear in the status bar and can be expanded to show more detail.

What's the Agenda?

If the day, week, and month views aren't your cup of tea, you're not alone. The month and week views can get cluttered and hard to read pretty quickly if you have more than three events per day (not as hard as it sounds). Fear not, fair reader! Google has a solution for that problem too: the Agenda (**Figure 4.22**).

Figure 4.22
*The Agenda list is
the most useful
Calendar view.*

The Agenda is essentially a list of all your upcoming events from all
synced calendars, displayed in a nice clean interface. It shows the name
of the event, the date(s), location, alarm, URL, repeating status (the
circling-arrows icon), and the calendar color. Touch an event in any view
to view and edit the event details (**Figure 4.23**).

Figure 4.23
*The Agenda's
event-details
screen.*

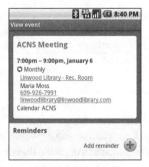

The Agenda is by far the easiest calendar view to read and use, which
is probably why it's the first option you see when you press the Menu

button in the Calendar app. You'll use it a lot. I rarely look at the other calendar views because it's so much quicker to flick and scroll through the Agenda.

Caveat Calendar

Like many other things in life, Google Calendar does have a couple of limitations:

- As with most Google applications, I find it quicker to do any substantial editing in the full version of the application on a desktop computer. For entering anything more than a few words, I'm much faster at typing on my full desktop keyboard than on any mobile device's keyboard, and nothing beats a big screen, especially for viewing a busy month in Google Calendar.

- At this writing, several features of the desktop version of Google Calendar haven't made it to the Android edition: sending invitations, creating calendars, sharing calendars, and adding a public calendar.

I wouldn't worry too much about these limitations, though. All the important features are in the Android edition now, and a lot of talented coders at Google headquarters are on the case. I wouldn't be surprised if Google Calendar could paint your house by the time you read this book.

That wraps up a pretty long chapter about the Droid's three core applications: Phone, Contacts, and Calendar. As with anything, you'll get more proficient with use, so it's important to embrace these core apps and put them to work for you. Time invested in them now will pay off in more free time in the future—or at least in fewer missed meetings.

In Chapter 5, I take a look at three other critical pieces of Droid software: email, messaging, and Web browsing.

5

Email, Messaging, and Web

Now that I've given you a look at three fundamental Droid apps (Phone, Contacts, and Calendar), it's time to turn your attention to three critical communication apps: Email, Messaging, and Web browsing.

Many people purchase a Droid specifically for its ability to send and receive email. Email is one of the defining features of a smartphone, and if your Droid has a QWERTY keyboard (sorry, Eris owners), you'll be tapping out emails almost as fast as you can on your desktop computer.

Even if you don't have a hardware keyboard, both the Droid and Droid Eris include software-based, onscreen keyboards. The software technology behind virtual keyboards like these is improving, and accuracy and speed are improving with every successive release of the Android operating system.

note A lot of development resources are being devoted to voice recognition, too, so look for a proliferation of applications that will accept and transcribe your voice in the not-too-distant future.

In this chapter, I jump-start your knowledge of Android's mail and messaging applications, take a close look at the practical use of these applications, and provide some tips and tricks for good measure. I round out the chapter with a look at the Droid's excellent Web browser, arguably the most powerful feature of any smartphone.

Email

The Droid allows you to take your email with you wherever you go, making it even more convenient than a desktop or even a notebook computer. Droid supports several types of email: corporate (Exchange 2003 and 2007), Gmail, IMAP, POP3 with full support for attachments, and Microsoft Office and Adobe PDF documents.

The Droid comes with two email applications, Gmail and Email (**Figure 5.1**)—and actually comes with three if you count the Web browser. The first is Google's popular Web-based email service, which is widely regarded as being one of the best; the second is a universal email client that you can use to access any email account based on POP3 or IMAP.

Figure 5.1
Android's Gmail and Email applications allow you to stay connected almost anywhere.

 note POP3 (Post Office Protocol, Version 3) and IMAP (Internet Message Access Protocol) are the dominant email protocols.

> **tip** Corporate email allows clients of Microsoft Exchange 2003 or 2007 servers to synchronize email, contacts, and calendars over the Droid's wireless Internet connection. Contact your company's IT department for the settings for your Exchange server.

Using Gmail

Google began offering Webmail service under the Gmail moniker publicly in 2007, although it was available as a private beta application as early as 2004. The service, whose official name is Google Mail, has more than 146 million monthly users, largely because of its simple yet powerful interface and high storage capacity (currently, more than 7 GB per account). It's also desirable for people who receive large attachments because a Gmail account will accept attachments as large as 25 MB—more than double the capacity of its competitors.

In addition to being intuitive enough for my 78-year-old mother-in-law to use, Gmail is loaded with features such as a powerful search feature (no surprise there!). It also provides a threaded view called *conversations* that allows you to see all messages with the same subject in one convenient screen without having to hunt through your inbox for previous messages on the same topic.

The main Gmail view is the inbox, which lists all your messages in reverse chronological order (**Figure 5.2**, on the next page).

The most powerful feature of Gmail in Android shows new messages in your inbox as they arrive without your having to refresh the inbox or check your email. This feature, called *push*, means that your Gmail inbox is up to date at all times.

Figure 5.2

The Gmail app's inbox.

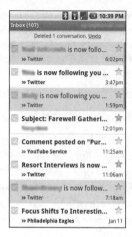

Launching the app

Because Gmail is tied to the Google account that you set up in Chapter 2, you don't have anything to configure. Just launch the application by touching its icon, and you'll be greeted by your inbox.

As you accumulate email in your account, you'll see your most recent email at the top of the main screen (your inbox). To see older emails, just drag your finger from the bottom to the top of the screen—a technique called *flicking*.

Reading an email is as simple as touching it in the inbox. When you do, you see the subject line, sender, and date, followed by the message itself.

note Great news! As of Android 2.0, the Gmail app is no longer limited to one Google account. Now you can set up multiple Gmail or Exchange accounts.

tip Android 2.0's new universal inbox allows you to view the latest email from all your accounts in one simple interface, which sure beats switching among multiple email accounts—a process that takes multiple touches.

Because Gmail can display HTML messages, emails are rendered beautifully on the Droid via *antialiasing,* a technology that generates smooth round edges and easy-to-read, eye-pleasing text. Touch the star to the right of the sender's email address to mark the message as a favorite, as you can do with contacts (see Chapter 4).

Viewing inbox options

Pressing the Menu button while you're viewing the inbox gives you access to the six options shown in **Figure 5.3**.

Figure 5.3
To access Gmail options, press the Menu button while you're viewing the inbox.

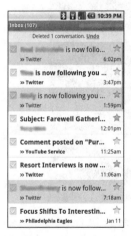

These options are

- **Refresh.** For the truly impatient, this option forces the inbox to refresh (although refreshing technically isn't required, thanks to Gmail's push feature).

- **Compose.** Touch this option to write a new email.

- **Accounts.** Touch this option to switch among multiple accounts or to add a new account.

- **View Labels.** This option, which is another way to filter your email, displays only email with a given label (see "Managing mail" later in this chapter).

- **Search.** This option allows you to search your email for a keyword or phrase.

- **Settings.** The Settings option gives you access to further options in the General Settings screen (**Figure 5.4**):

Figure 5.4
Gmail's general settings allow you to do things like add a signature and receive a status-bar notification when you get new email.

Signature. Allows you to add a custom footer to messages that you compose. Usually, a signature contains contact information.

Confirm Delete. Displays a confirmation dialog box when you mark an email for deletion (see "Managing mail" later in this chapter).

Batch Operations. Allows you to apply labels to multiple email conversations.

Clear Search History. Removes all the searches that you've performed.

Labels. Lets you specify which labels are synchronized to your Droid.

 Email Notifications. Displays a status-bar icon when you receive a new email.

 I highly recommend that you keep this option enabled; it's super-convenient.

Select Ringtone. Plays a ringtone when a new email arrives. (I prefer to keep my Droid silent due to the volume of email that I receive.)

Vibrate. Sets your phone to vibrate when a new email arrives.

Managing mail

Here's a little trick that saves me a lot of time: Long-press a message in the inbox view to access email options without having to open the message. These options are

- **Read.** Allows you to read the message as though you'd touched it normally. (I know—duh!)

- **Archive.** Moves messages out of your inbox, letting you tidy up your inbox without deleting anything.

- **Mute.** Keeps your inbox free of unwanted threads. Here's how: When you *mute* a message, follow-up emails to the conversation bypass the inbox. If you're being copied on a thread that doesn't involve you (or that you'd like to ignore), touch Mute.

- **Mark Read.** Allows you to mark a message as being read without having to touch it to do so. This feature is more useful than it sounds and is quicker than loading the whole message.

- **Delete.** Removes a message or conversation from Gmail—eventually. *Delete* is actually a misnomer here. When you delete an email in Android, it's actually stashed in the Trash folder on the Droid for 30 days; *then* it's deleted.

tip Deleting can free some of your storage, but with Gmail's free storage, it's best to keep all your emails. If you just want to get an email out of your face, I recommend using the Archive option instead.

- **Add/Remove Star.** Adds a star next to certain messages or conversations to give them special status, or removes said star. Starred items remain visible when you return to a conversation.

- **Change Labels.** Changes the label attached to a particular email. Think of labels as being folders with a bonus: You can add more than one label to an email. In your inbox, press the Menu button and then touch Labels (see the preceding section) to narrow your email view.

- **Report Spam.** Allows you to report a message as spam without opening it. When you do, the offending pork product is removed from your inbox, and you help Google prevent more like it from arriving.

Using the Email application

Not everyone chooses Gmail as his or her email provider, because most people had another email account before Gmail came along. To serve non-Gmail users, Google includes a more generic Email application on the Droid that lets you access an unlimited number of POP3 and/or IMAP accounts.

Setting up the Email app on the Droid couldn't be easier, thanks to a convenient wizard that walks you through the process the first time you launch the application.

note Before you embark on this little journey, you have to provide some information, such as your password, incoming and outgoing email servers, and any special ports. It's best to assemble this information before you start.

Setting up your account

To set up your account by using the Email application's setup wizard, follow these steps:

1. Enter your email address and password (**Figure 5.5**); then touch Next.

   If you enter an address from a popular Webmail service such as Yahoo or Hotmail, the wizard automatically completes most of the settings for you—a nice feature.

Figure 5.5
Email's setup wizard first asks for your address and password.

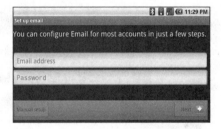

> **tip** If you're an expert, you can dispense with the wizard and enter your settings in one dense screen by touching Manual Setup in the bottom-left corner of the first wizard screen.

2. In the next screen, touch the button for your email account type (**Figure 5.6**).

Figure 5.6
Choose the account type that you want to set up.

If you're not sure whether your account is POP3 or IMAP, you'll have to ask your Internet service provider (ISP) or the IT staff at your company. If no one is available, try POP3 first. (Even though I prefer IMAP, many providers default to POP3 unless you specifically request an IMAP account.)

3. In the next screen, enter your incoming server settings, including your user name, password, server, port, and security type (**Figure 5.7**); then touch Next.

Figure 5.7
Enter your incoming server settings here.

Your user name usually is the first part of your email address, but some ISPs require your complete address as your user name. The IMAP server (or POP3 server) can be anything your ISP desires. Some of the most popular servers simply append *imap.* or *mail.* to the beginning of your domain name, but check with your ISP or the IT folks if you don't know.

tip Instead of waiting on hold with technical support to get your email settings, try checking the incoming and outgoing account information in your desktop computer's email application. You can glean most of the neces- sary settings there, although your password will be bulleted out. If you can't remember your password, you may have to make that call.

4. Enter your outgoing server settings in the next screen (**Figure 5.8**); then touch Next.

Figure 5.8
Enter your outgoing server settings here.

The Outgoing Server Settings screen is slightly more complicated than its incoming counterpart due to the Security Type drop-down menu. My ISP requires Secure Sockets Layer (SSL) authentication, so I choose the SSL option from this menu, but your mileage may vary. Check with your email provider for its specific outgoing security type.

note Thanks to the scourge of spam, ISPs have been forced to add security to their outgoing mail servers. The user name and password you enter here usually are the same ones that you use for your email account, but definitely check with your ISP if you're not sure.

5. Set a few options in the Account Options screen (**Figure 5.9**) and then touch Next:

Figure 5.9
This screen allows you to set things like your email checking frequency.

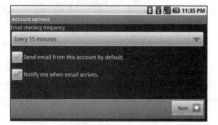

- **Frequency of checking email.** This setting is a personal preference. Being a data nut (and somewhat obsessive), I usually choose the shortest checking frequency—in this case, 15 minutes. If Gmail had a setting for 15 *seconds*, I would choose that.

- **Default account.** If this account is the primary account that you want to send email from, check the top check box.

@ ■ **Notification method.** To have Gmail display an icon in the status bar when a new email arrives, check the bottom check box.

note One really nice aspect of getting email notification in the status bar is that in addition to displaying the email icon, the status bar displays the first several words of the incoming message's Subject line.

6. In the next screen (**Figure 5.10**), name your account so that you can distinguish it from others; enter your real name in the second field (which will be displayed as the "From" address on email that you send); and then touch Done.

Figure 5.10
Give your email account a name, and you're off to the races!

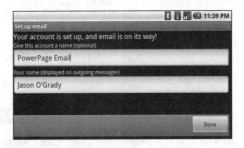

If all went well, you see your inbox (**Figure 5.11**), with your most recent emails listed (sender's address, subject line, and date). It's easy to miss, but a vertical green bar on the left edge of the screen indicates an unread message. After you touch a message to read it, the green bar goes away.

Figure 5.11
The email inbox.

A green bar marks —
unread messages.

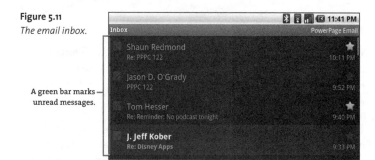

tip   **Long-pressing an email in the inbox reveals a drop-down box
that allows you to open, delete, forward, reply all, reply, or mark
as unread in one quick step.**

Reading, replying, and composing

Assuming that you didn't jump right to this section from the table of
contents, you can probably guess how to do most of the things associated with email. Reading, replying to, and composing emails are
extremely intuitive tasks on the Droid, and most functions are only
a screen touch away.

You handle pretty much everything else by pressing the Menu button
and then touching the desired icon (refer to Figure 5.3 earlier in this
chapter). Rather than repeat all that information here (this book is
a *Pocket Guide,* after all!), I refer you to the "Viewing inbox options" and
"Managing mail" sections of the Gmail topic earlier in this chapter.

There you have it. Your email is popping!

Messaging

Whether you're tweenaged or in your 60s, you've probably figured out by now that text messaging is the new email. In fact, it's the new voice mail and the new everything else these days, at least when it comes to mobile phones.

The extreme convenience of text messaging has undoubtedly contributed to its meteoric rise in popularity over the past decade. It's used by approximately 75 percent of mobile-phone subscribers, translating into 2.4 billion active users and 15 billion messages sent each year. Whew!

Sending messages via Short Message Service (SMS), or just *texting*, is ideal for those times when you want to convey a message that's not long enough for an email or important enough to justify a phone call. It's also handy for times when you don't want to disrupt the recipient with a phone call but can't wait for him to check his email.

Because they're limited to 160 characters (about 25 words, give or take), text messages force you to summarize what you could probably talk about for 20 minutes on the phone or ramble on about for 11 paragraphs in an email. For many people, this very brevity makes texting so powerful—and it doesn't hurt that most phones (including the Droid) notify you when you have an SMS message via an in-your-face alert.

Like all good technologies, SMS got an upgrade in 2002 to Multimedia Messaging Service (MMS), which allows users to send longer messages and include images, audio, video, and rich text. It's most popular for sending photos from camera-equipped phones.

The Droid comes with both SMS and MMS in one convenient application called Messaging. In the following sections, I go over some of the features of both types of messaging, so stretch those thumbs; they're about to get a workout.

tip   If you get bitten by the texting bug, you need to invest in an unlimited text package. It's easy to exceed the number of text messages included in your plan (if you get any, that is), and at 20 cents per outgoing or incoming message, overages can add up quickly. If you have teenage children, just buck up for the unlimited plan, as you'll probably be texting them when dinner is ready.

Short Message Service

The beauty of SMS is its simplicity—no complicated configuration, no difficult settings, and frankly not much to learn. You start using it by launching the Messaging application with a simple touch. When the application loads, you see the Messaging inbox, displaying the messages you've received in reverse chronological order (**Figure 5.12**). Like the Gmail and Email applications, which I cover earlier in this chapter, Messaging displays a green vertical bar on the left edge of unread messages.

Figure 5.12
The messaging inbox isn't much different from the email inbox—just a little spiffier, thanks to the picture thumbnails.

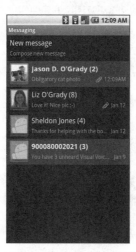

The first 35 characters of received messages are visible in the inbox view, along with the sender, time, and date. If the sender is in your contact list (see Chapter 4 for more on contacts), you'll see her proper name displayed; if not, you see just her mobile-phone number. Messages sent from your carrier (such as the one from 900080002021 in Figure 5.12) often display partial numbers and don't accept replies. Fortunately, carriers usually don't charge for these messages.

The quickest way to compose a message is to touch the first line of the Messaging inbox, labeled New Message. Another way is to press the Menu button, touch the Compose icon, enter a contact's name (or phone number) in the To field, write a message, and then press the Send button.

When you receive a text or multimedia message, a notification icon in the status bar tells you so. Slide the status bar down and touch the message to go directly to the Messaging app's detail view (**Figure 5.13**), where you can view the entire conversation (if any) and reply to the sender. Touching any message in the inbox also takes you to detail view.

Figure 5.13

The messaging detail view displays the sender's thumbnail image, plus any inline MMS objects, like the photo in this thread.

To set SMS options, press the Menu button and then touch Settings. The Settings screen (**Figure 5.14**) contains several options that are pretty self-explanatory, thanks to the help text below each option.

Figure 5.14
The Messaging app's Settings screen lists a variety of useful options.

tip The coolest feature of SMS and MMS messages is the Delivery Reports option. When you enable this option, the Droid sends you a message to confirm that your outgoing message reached its destination—similar to a return receipt from the post office. Unfortunately, this feature isn't a perfect science, so don't rely on it to be 100 accurate.

Multimedia Messaging Service

Multimedia Messaging Service (MMS) is the next generation of SMS. In addition to sending a vanilla text message, you can attach images, audio, video, and rich text, so comparing MMS with SMS is like comparing a banana split with a vanilla cone. A better analogy would be comparing SMS and MMS with plain text and HTML emails.

Although MMS is super-useful for sending photos from camera-equipped phones (like both Droids), it can also be annoying when you go off the deep end and send a birthday card that includes an animated singing frog. As with most things in life, discretion is the better part of valor when it comes to MMS.

To send an MMS, touch New Message at the top of the Messaging inbox (refer to Figure 5.12 earlier in this chapter), or touch Menu > Compose. Add a recipient and some text; then touch Menu > Attach. The resulting screen (**Figure 5.15**) allows you to attach pictures, audio, video, and slideshows.

Figure 5.15
MMS trumps SMS with its support of attachments. It also allows you to send a picture to a friend instantly.

note Before you go hog-wild sending all kinds of fancy media attachments, make sure that your recipient can accept MMS messages. If he can't, he'll get a strange message asking him to log in to a Web page to retrieve it. If you're not certain that your recipient has an MMS-capable phone, send an SMS message instead.

Twitter: The New IM?

If texting is the new email, Twitter is arguably the new instant messaging (IM). I haven't used IM since switching almost exclusively to Twitter in early 2007—but that's a story for another chapter, my friend! For more Twitter fun, download Twidroid Pro. It's my favorite Twitter app for Android, and I cover it in Chapter 8.

Web Browsing

By this point in the book, I hope that I don't have to explain the power of the Web. Because you've invested in a Droid (or are considering investing in one), you're probably a pretty Web-savvy person. Because my cats are fairly proficient at using the Web (maybe *that's* where those preapproved credit-card offers are coming from!), I'd like to assume that you are too.

That said, the World Wide Web gives you access to more information than kings and rulers of land had as little as 100 years ago. The Web is a much faster way to get information, too. Rather than having to dispatch a legion of serfs across land and sea to gather information, you can simply type a few keywords in Google, and boom!—thousands of results (or even millions) are at your disposal. Results are returned in milliseconds, rather than days/weeks/months or even years. What did we do before Google?

In all seriousness, the importance, utility, and convenience of the Web are irrefutable. The Web allows you to research a book (ahem!); get prices, reviews, and dealer costs for just about anything; conduct online banking; attend meetings; and buy and sell all kinds of items. On the Droid, you start by touching the Browser icon.

Mobile browsers

Although expectations can be high, it's important to understand that mobile Web browsers aren't perfect. You're limited to a small screen and keyboard, and you have less memory and storage. Another important limitation of the Droid is that the browser can't display Adobe Flash content. Otherwise, mobile-phone browsers operate pretty much like the browsers on desktop computers. You can zoom in, zoom out, and move inside a Web page.

tip The first smartphone to come with support for Flash was the HTC Hero, released June 24, 2009. Although it's not available for Droid as of February 2010, Adobe Flash Player 10.1 is coming to Android 2.0 and future releases in the first half of 2010.

Odds are that you've used a browser before (yes?), so I won't go into detail on the basics of a Web address and the like. Instead, I'll focus on how a mobile browser differs from a desktop Web browser.

First, though, some technical background is in order. Google uses WebKit as its browser in Android. (This application framework also powers Apple's Safari and Nokia's S60 browser.) Although WebKit does an adequate job of rendering complex Web pages, it can be slow at times. Like all good technologies, it will get better over time.

The Droid browser

To use the Droid's Web browser, simply touch the aptly named Browser icon. The browser displays a cached version of the last page you were browsing. To navigate to a Web page, just touch the search/URL field at the top of the screen (**Figure 5.16**); type the Web address that you want to visit; and touch Go.

Figure 5.16

The Droid browser. To display the six options at the bottom of the screen, press the Menu button.

> **tip** If you don't feel like typing, just touch the microphone icon to the right of the search field and simply speak your query. Google will transcribe your commands and execute a search. No clicking whatsoever is involved. This feature isn't just cool; it's revolutionary.

> **tip** If you're not sure of the Web address, you can enter a search term in the search field (such as *Droid Pocket Guide*), and you'll get search results from Google. You can also touch the Search button to do the same thing.

You have several ways to navigate a Web page, but I find the most convenient to be simply dragging a finger around on the touchscreen. When you're browsing a page that's too large for the Droid's screen (which isn't easy!), simply rotate it to use the wider landscape format. I find it a little easier to read long Web pages in landscape mode, but you should experiment with both portrait and landscape modes to see which works better for you.

If you're browsing a Web page that's not optimized for the small screen, touching anywhere on the screen displays two small magnifying-glass icons at the bottom of the screen (**Figure 5.17**). As you've probably guessed, you touch the plus (+) and minus (–) icons to zoom in and out of a Web page, respectively.

Figure 5.17
Viewing a Web page gives you two buttons for zooming in and out. It's not quite multitouch, but it'll do.

Zoom out ——— ——— Zoom in

Double-tap anywhere on a Web page to zoom into that particular area for closer viewing. When you're finished with a particular section, double-tap again to zoom back out to your previous view.

note Although the Droids don't ship with multitouch support in the United States, curiously, the Motorola Milestone (which has the same hardware as the Droid) ships with multitouch features in the United Kingdom. This means that the Droid itself isn't the limitation. Look for multitouch to roll out to all Android devices eventually—say, when the deal between Eric Schmidt and Steve Jobs expires.

Shopping on the Run

When you're using the browser to search Google, you see a new icon to the right of the Search button—an icon that looks like a minia-ture bar code (Figure 5.18). If you touch it, you can download a free Android application called Barcode Scanner, which lets you use the Droid's camera to scan bar codes and then look up product informa-tion such as prices and reviews.

Figure 5.18

Tapping the mini bar-code icon to the right of the search field allows you to scan a bar code with your Droid's camera. Talk about cool!

Bar-code icon

Bookmarks, windows, and settings

The Android Web browser functions just like a desktop browser, right down to the bookmarks. Rather than touch the same Web address over and over, create a bookmark, which is much faster. To bookmark the page that you're viewing, touch Menu > More > Add Bookmark.

To navigate to a page that you've already bookmarked, press the Menu button and then touch Bookmarks (refer to Figure 5.16 earlier in this chapter). The browser displays your bookmarks in reverse chronological order, including a handy thumbnail image of the Web page (**Figure 5.19**). To go to a bookmark, simply touch it or (on the Droid Eris) select and click it with the trackball.

Figure 5.19
Bookmarks view displays convenient thumbnail images.

If you're a power browser, having several browser windows open at the same time is convenient. Unfortunately, the Droid's screen isn't large enough for browser tabs. Instead, a built-in Windows feature allows you to navigate up to four Web pages quickly and easily (**Figure 5.20**). To access this feature, press the Menu button and then touch Windows (refer to Figure 5.16 earlier in this chapter). Touch any page that you see in the Windows screen to go to that page, or touch the New Window option in the top-left corner to go to a different page.

Rounding out the browser's menu options are Refresh, which reloads the page that you're viewing (which can be helpful when tickets for Phish at Red Rocks are about to go on sale); and More, which reveals navigation options and functions for sharing, bookmarking, and viewing a page's information (**Figure 5.21**).

Figure 5.20
The Windows screen lists all the Web pages that you have open.

Figure 5.21
Touching the Browser app's More icon displays a litany of options, such as these.

Settings Galore

If you're into tweaking settings, you'll be in heaven when you touch Menu > More > Settings in the Android browser. The resulting Settings screen is easily the longest I've seen in any Android application (four scrolls!) and rivals the settings screen in most desktop browsers.

The first section, which covers the page-content settings, allows you to set the text size and things like pop-up blocking and loading images. For the most part, I leave these settings alone.

The second section focuses on privacy settings; it allows you to clear the cache, history, and cookies. The Remember Form Data option is extremely helpful, because it saves you from having to enter the same information (such as your user name and password) on pages that you visit frequently.

The Security section allows you to remember and clear passwords. (Saving form data isn't recommended for sensitive sites such as banking and e-commerce, because if you lose your phone, the person who finds it can look through your history and bookmarks, as well as log in to your accounts. Never save logins for sensitive sites on your Droid.)

The Advanced section allows you to enable and customize Google Gears. This app allows you to extend the browser's functionality by saving pages for offline viewing, which is eminently useful at times when you may be without Internet connectivity, such as when you're on a commercial flight. Gears allows you to keep working when most people are forced to play solitaire.

Google Maps Navigation

The advent of Google Maps Navigation means never having to use paper maps again—provided that you don't run out of battery power, that is! With this app, you can determine your current location, find businesses and landmarks, get driving directions and real-time traffic reports, and explore satellite and street images.

Google Maps Navigation is a major upgrade of an already amazing app. Whereas the older version simply displayed your location and gave directions, the new version (**Figure 6.1**, on the next page) takes things up a notch by adding turn-by-turn, voice-guided navigation.

note It's easy to confuse the new Google Maps Navigation app with the old Google Maps app. For simplicity, I'll call the new app *Google Maps* or *Maps* in this chapter. Just keep in mind that I'm talking about Google Maps Navigation unless I state otherwise.

Figure 6.1
*Google Maps
is now a
full-featured
navigation
system.*

The new features in Google Maps transform the Droid into a powerful navigation device that could easily replace the Global Positioning System (GPS) receiver currently sitting on your dash. In fact, I'd bet that executives at companies like Garmin, TomTom, and Magellan are losing sleep over it.

note The navigation features included in Google Maps are for use in the United States only. If you're looking for navigation elsewhere, you can find several international apps in the Android Market (see Chapter 8); just search for *navigation*.

Google Maps can even take advantage of the accelerometer built into the Droid to know which way you're holding or tilting the phone, which allows you to see not only your location—to an accuracy of about 10 feet (3 meters)—but also the direction in which you're facing. This feature saves a lot of time and takes the guesswork out of determining your heading. It's pretty powerful stuff.

You'll probably use Google Maps for four main functions: finding locations, getting directions, navigating, and sharing your location. I cover each function in detail in this chapter. In addition, I give you a tour of the application's new, experimental Labs feature.

note **The new Google Maps Navigation app is available only for devices running Android 2.0 or later. As of press time, this group did *not* include the Droid Eris. Not to worry, though—Verizon has announced that it plans to release Android 2.0 for the Droid Eris in the first quarter of 2010. The software should be available via an Over the Air (OTA) update by the time you read this book.**

Set Your Location

Before GPS satellites can locate your Droid, you have to give them explicit permission to do so. This permission requirement is a way to protect your privacy. (Not everyone wants to be able to be found to within 10 feet at all times, after all.) To use the GPS features of the Droid, you have to touch Settings > Locations & Security and check the Use GPS Satellites box in the resulting screen (**Figure 6.2**).

Figure 6.2
The My Location screen allows you to toggle GPS on and off.

tip The Use GPS Satellites setting is extremely accurate, but the trade-off is that it uses a lot of battery power when it's enabled. If you need to conserve your battery, GPS is the first thing that you should turn off.

In case you're wondering, the Use Wireless Networks setting at the top of Figure 6.2 uses cell towers and Wi-Fi networks to locate your phone. Although this option uses less battery power than the GPS option does, it's also less accurate than GPS.

Find a Location

Launch Google Maps by touching its icon, and you'll see the last map you viewed. If you have GPS turned on, Maps will pinpoint your current location and display it on a map. If not, press the Menu button and then touch My Location (**Figure 6.3**).

Figure 6.3
The My Location option is displayed when you press Menu.

To find an address or city, touch Menu > Search. In the resulting screen (**Figure 6.4**), enter an address, business, or city, or simply touch the microphone icon and speak your query. If you say "pizza," for example, Maps returns all the pizza shops near you, neatly plotted as a series of small red dots on your map. After touching one of the results, you get options to call the phone number, view the location on a map, get directions, or navigate to it. Pizza indeed! (I cover voice search in more detail in the next section.)

Figure 6.4
The search option in Maps also displays your search history.

Touch this icon to search by voice.

> **tip** When searching for an address that you've found before, you don't need to retype. Just type the first few letters and then choose the address from the drop-down list below the search box.

Google has also improved the business listings that appear in the search results to include content such as store hours, prices, ratings, and reviews.

Voice search

Google Maps' voice search is an extremely powerful feature that allows you to speak your destination instead of typing it. It employs the same core voice-search technology that's used in other areas of the Android operating system, which is best in class and accurate enough to be used as the primary interface to the device. I probably speak more search terms and addresses to my Droid than I type because speaking is faster and more convenient.

To use voice search, follow these steps:

1. Make sure that your Droid has an active Internet connection (see Chapter 5).

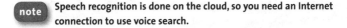 **Speech recognition is done on the cloud, so you need an Internet connection to use voice search.**

2. Touch the microphone icon (refer to Figure 6.4), and say what you want to search for.

   You could say something like "Navigate to the Cape May Lewis Ferry," for example.

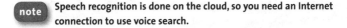 **My experience has been that the Droid's speech recognition is excellent, understanding American, Australian, and British English. (At this writing, voice search is available only in English.)**

   When Maps finishes searching, it displays the result plotted on a map or—in the event of multiple choices—a list of results.

3. If the result shown onscreen is correct, follow the voice guidance; if you get multiple results, simply touch the proper result in the list and then follow the voice guidance.

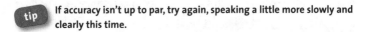 **If accuracy isn't up to par, try again, speaking a little more slowly and clearly this time.**

Layers

The Layers feature displays different types of data over the top of a traditional Google map. To access it, touch the Maps icon and then touch the

Layers icon at the bottom of the screen (refer to Figure 6.3 earlier in this chapter).

Figure 6.5 shows the Layers screen, which offers options including the following:

Figure 6.5
Layers allows you to choose how you want to view maps.

- **Traffic.** Traffic view displays real-time traffic conditions (where available) on the roads as color-coded lines. For more details on this feature, see the "Traffic" section later in this chapter.

- **Satellite.** This view superimposes a map on an aerial photo.

- **Latitude.** Latitude view displays friends' locations on a map. I cover this feature later in the last section of the chapter.

Touching the More Layers button (bottom of Figure 6.5) allows you to add even more layers for things like Wikipedia, Transit Lines, My Maps, and Favorite Places. Experiment with these options; they're a lot of fun. Just remember to come back and turn them off when they're no longer needed; they can clutter a map quickly.

Get Directions

Google Maps for Droid includes several types of directions, including driving, public transportation, and walking. I cover all these direction types in the following sections and also discuss an important aspect of travel: traffic.

Driving

If you've used Google Maps on your desktop computer, using Maps' Directions feature on your Droid will be second nature to you. To get driving directions, just follow these steps:

1. Touch the Maps icon to open the Maps screen.

2. Touch the Directions button at the bottom of the screen (refer to Figure 6.3 earlier in this chapter).

3. Enter your starting and ending locations in the two fields at the top of the screen (**Figure 6.6**).

Figure 6.6

Getting directions is as easy as entering two locations.

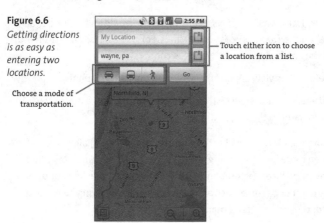

Touch either icon to choose a location from a list.

Choose a mode of transportation.

tip Touch the square icon to the right of each address field to choose a location source quickly. Your choices are **My Current Location**, **Contacts**, and **Point on Map** (*Figure 6.7*). Sure beats having to enter that same data by hand.

Figure 6.7
Choosing a location source instead of entering it saves time.

4. Touch the car icon.

5. Touch the Go button.

    A new screen opens (**Figure 6.8**, on the next page), giving you the option to view your destination on a map as a checkerboard pin, navigate to it (I cover navigation later in the chapter), or review the directions as a traditional text-based list.

Figure 6.8
Follow the onscreen directions or touch Navigate to get turn-by-turn instructions.

Public transportation

Getting directions for taking public transportation (**Figure 6.9**) is just as easy as getting them for driving a car. Just follow the procedure in the "Driving" section, but instead of touching the car icon in step 4, touch the bus icon (refer to Figure 6.6). When you touch the Go button, Maps routes you to your destination via available public transportation (trains, subways, buses, and so on).

Transit information isn't available everywhere, but I'm sure that Google is hard at work on expanding coverage. For more information on Google Maps for Transit, visit www.google.com/transit.

 Public-transit information is also available in the Maps app via a layer, which I cover in the "Layers" section earlier in this chapter.

Figure 6.9
Maps even provides transit directions, including transfers.

Walking

Most city centers are a maze of one-way and no-left-turn streets, so traditional driving directions rarely show the most direct route for traveling by foot. That's where your Droid comes in handy. To get walking directions, enter your start and end locations in the Directions screen (refer to Figure 6.6), touch the pedestrian icon, and then touch the Go button.

Walking directions are even more convenient than you may think, especially for short trips in urban areas, but they aren't perfect. Google doesn't always know where the sidewalks are, for example, and construction crews always seem to be working on the roads in my area. As with any output from a computer, take walking directions with a grain of salt, and sanity-check them against your own experience and common sense.

Traffic

The Layers screen (refer to Figure 6.5) offers you several ways to view your maps, but the Traffic layer is where the power of Google Maps really shines. When data is available, Google Maps provides live and predictive traffic information for all U.S. highways and secondary roads around the clock (**Figure 6.10**).

Figure 6.10

The Traffic layer indicates congestion by displaying green, yellow, and red lines on a map.

note Green, yellow, and red traffic alerts don't translate well to a book that contains black-and-white images, so you'll have to test this feature on your own.

This information is based on past conditions and live crowdsourcing, in which other Google Maps users anonymously send their speed and location information to Google in the background. I provide more details on traffic in the following section.

Navigate

Google Maps (**Figure 6.11**) provides free turn-by-turn GPS navigation with voice guidance, and it's Internet-connected around the clock to boot.

Figure 6.11
*Google Maps'
new navigation
feature is one of
the best reasons
to own a Droid.*

Although it's getting darned close, Google Maps isn't a perfect replacement for a dedicated GPS receiver for heavy navigation users. For starters,
the Droid's 3.7-inch-diagonal screen isn't as large as the screens that ship
in many modern GPS units, some of which are up to 5 inches diagonally.
Also, there's a definite advantage to having your phone separate from
your GPS receiver (although you *can* talk on the phone and navigate on
the Droid at the same time).

Constant Internet connection

According to Google, fewer than 1 percent of all GPS receivers are
constantly Internet-connected, and in my experience, those that are
charge a monthly fee for the service. (Dash.net, for example, charges
$13 per month for its Internet-connected GPS receiver.) Being Internet-
connected all the time means that you always have access to the latest
Google Maps data on your Droid.

Traditional GPS devices come with a set of maps that were installed at
the factory. If you purchase a GPS receiver in 2010, it could have maps

from 2009 or 2008 installed—and if you bought the device at a deep-discount or closeout sale, or bought it used, the maps will certainly be even older. It's important to have up-to-date maps, though, for at least a couple of reasons:

- Roads and subdivisions are always being closed, changed, or repaired (seemingly at the most inopportune times!).

- Business data—known as Points of Interest (POIs) in GPS parlance—is best served fresh. Although it may be inconvenient to find out that a road has been changed, it's much more inconvenient to discover that the gas station that you just navigated to closed years ago.

tip Maps' Internet connection is especially helpful when you're calling for a dinner reservation, as restaurants tend to turn over faster than most other businesses do.

Google Maps on your Droid is pulling data from the same giant database as good old Google.com on your desktop computer, so when you search for, say, a mechanic or emergency services, you can be sure that you have the most up-to-date information possible.

Several times, POIs that were in my GPS receiver (which had up-to-date maps, mind you) mysteriously weren't there when I drove to them. I learned a valuable lesson in the process: not to rely on the POI listings in my GPS receiver. With Google Maps , though, I don't feel compelled to call ahead to make sure that the business I'm looking for is still *in business*.

tip For mission-critical routes to doctors and hospitals, it never hurts to (ahem!) get a second opinion.

tip If the navigation features included in Google Maps are too pedestrian (pun intended) for you, you can find several alternative apps by searching for *navigation* in the Android Market (see Chapter 8). Be warned, though: These apps aren't free.

Traffic detection and avoidance

Google Maps can display real-time traffic data overlaid on top of maps in a simple green, yellow, and red color scheme. As with traffic lights, green means go (no traffic), yellow means slow down (some traffic), and red means stop (heavy traffic). To get details on an area, touch it to zoom out to an aerial view that shows traffic speeds and incidents ahead.

Google Maps gathers its traffic data via crowdsourcing, analyzing the speed and location data sent by other Maps users and turning that data into easy-to-read traffic data that benefits all users.

In addition to showing you traffic that's coming up on your route (detection), Google Maps can help you detour around it (avoidance). When Maps finds traffic on your route, it displays an alternative-route icon at the bottom of the screen (**Figure 6.12**). Touch that icon to display a new route around the traffic ahead.

Figure 6.12
The alternative-route icon allows you to detour around traffic.

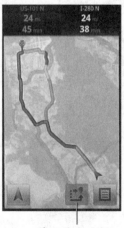

Alternative-route icon

Satellite view

Although it's not just for navigation, satellite view is one of Google's most popular features, because it shows you very accurately where you're going, and also helps you put your route in context by displaying landmarks like parks, buildings, and bodies of water.

To enable this feature, simply touch the Layers icon (refer to Figure 6.3 earlier in this chapter), or touch Menu > Layers and then touch Satellite. Instead of seeing a boring, line-art map devoid of detail, you'll see a view of your location as only a satellite can show it (**Figure 6.13**).

Figure 6.13
Satellite view is more useful on a smartphone than on a desktop computer.

Satellite view won't clog the precious storage on your Droid; all the data is downloaded on demand from Google via your Internet connection. James Bond would be proud.

Street View

Street View (**Figure 6.14**) allows you to take a virtual drive or walk down most major U.S. streets, thanks to street-level photos that Google has painstakingly collected and mapped to GPS coordinates. The result is fantastically useful for finding a specific personal or business destination, scouting locations for a trip or film, or even finding a new home—all without ever leaving your current zip code.

Figure 6.14
Street View can be amazingly helpful on a Droid.

Although some other GPS receivers show you an artist's rendering of a particular road or street sign, Google Maps on the Droid shows you actual street-level photos of your route so that you can plan your next turn easily (or find a place to park). When you arrive at your destination, Google Maps also shows you a Street View of the location, making sure that you arrive at the right place and not at the building next door.

Street View is available on desktop computers, but it becomes even more powerful when it's used on a mobile device like the Droid. It's one thing to use Street View to scout a hotel before you book it from your office PC, but it's even more useful when you're trying to find the location of your business meeting while you're on foot (with your Droid, of course!).

Car-dock mode (Droid only)

note Car-dock mode is not available for the Droid Eris.

If you're going to use Google Maps in your vehicle (and who wouldn't?), you should make one additional purchase: a good car dock that lets you safely mount your Droid on your vehicle's windshield. Having a car dock beats having a Droid slide across your dashboard; trust me on that one.

Luckily, Motorola has released the Car Mount for Droid ($30), a suction-cup mounting bracket that attaches to said windshield and gives you a slide-in bracket for your Droid. When you snap your Droid into the mount, the device switches to car-dock mode (**Figure 6.15**).

Figure 6.15
Car-dock mode turns the Droid into a full-fledged personal navigation device.

Car-dock mode is an excellent software feature that optimizes the Droid's interface for arm's-length control, displaying large icons that are easy to read (and touch) from a distance. It also boils the Droid interface down to five main tasks:

- View Map
- Navigation
- Voice Search
- Contacts
- Search

note Car-dock mode also provides a (small) Home icon for the times when you need something other than the Big Five features.

The icon for the single best feature of car-dock mode—voice search—is placed front and center. As I discuss in copious detail elsewhere in this chapter and book, voice search allows you to speak instead of type your query. Nowhere is this type of feature more valuable than in car-dock mode, because when you're driving, you should have your hands on the wheel and your eyes on the road.

To use it, simply touch the Voice Search icon, and when you're prompted, say a phrase like "Navigate to Armadillo Willy's" (**Figure 6.16**). Google Maps displays that phrase and maps your route. If it heard you right, that's all you have to do. If the text onscreen isn't what you said, touch the Cancel button and try again.

Figure 6.16

Navigating by voice in car-dock mode allows you to simply speak your destination.

Voice-activated features aren't infallible, because they can be adversely affected by things like background noise, but after you get used to them, there's simply no going back. What could be easier than speaking to your computer or phone? (I guess thinking instead of speaking would be a little easier, but that's a topic for another *Pocket Guide*.)

Share with Latitude

Google Maps is handy for more than just viewing maps and providing directions; it's also excellent for sharing your current location with friends. Sharing is the basis of a whole new category of social-networking applications, and Google is joining the party with its own entry.

Google Latitude (www.google.com/latitude) is a social-networking service that plots your friends' locations on a map (**Figure 6.17**)—a handy way to see who's out and about. With it, you can text, instant-message, or call any of your friends who are nearby. This feature is only as good as the number of your friends who use it, so to make it successful, you need to invite your friends to share your data and hope that they reciprocate.

Figure 6.17
With Latitude, it's easy to see when your friends are in the area.

If you're concerned about stalkers, keep in mind that Latitude is an opt-in feature, which means that *you* turn it on and *you* determine who can see your location. For obvious reasons, exercise a lot of discretion in sharing your location information, and grant access only to your closest friends.

To participate in Latitude, you need to join. To do so, touch Menu > Join Latitude; then touch Menu > Add Friends, and select people from your contacts list or add people's email addresses manually. When you're done, those people will receive an email invitation to Latitude.

note **You can remove a friend by long-pressing his name and then touching Remove This Friend in the resulting list.**

Sharing your location . . .

Latitude periodically asks you to share your location details with another user. When it does, you have three choices:

- **Accept and Share Back.** When you choose this option, you can see your friends' locations, and they can see yours.

- **Accept, but Hide My Location.** This option lets you see your friends' locations but blocks them from seeing yours.

- **Don't Accept.** You can't see your friends, and they can't see you.

. . . or not

You can stop publishing your location information to your Latitude friends at any time by touching Menu > Privacy in the main Latitude screen. This screen gives you four options:

- **Detect Your Location.** This option (the default) updates your location automatically.

- **Set Your Location.** When you choose this option, you set your location on the map manually.

- **Hide Your Location.** Choose this option, and your friends can't see your location.

- **Turn off Latitude.** When you turn off Latitude, you can't see or be seen.

Experiment with Labs

Although the name conjures images of serious-looking academics in lab coats using Bunsen burners (at least, it does for me), Labs is a fun experimental area of Google where programmers are allowed to test new software on us. Wait a minute—they're experimenting on us! Stop the presses!

Seriously, though, the Labs feature of Google Maps has some pretty amazing features, and I'm baffled as to why they're not in the main screen. To view these features (**Figure 6.18**), touch Menu > More > Labs.

note As with anything new, experimental, or from Google, expect Labs to change. The features that I discuss in the following sections were available on my Droid running Android 2.0.1 and Maps 3.3.1 in January 2010. At the rate at which technology is progressing, Labs may also have an option to make you a sandwich by the time you read this book.

Figure 6.18
Lurking in Google Maps are several experimental features that are quite exciting and useful.

Scale bar

The Scale Bar option displays a scale (both imperial and metric units) in the bottom-left corner of a map. It's really useful for telling the distance between two locations, especially if you zoom in and out of maps frequently.

Terrain layer

The Terrain Layer option lets you view physical features such as mountains and vegetation, along with elevation shading (**Figure 6.19**). It's super-useful for planning your next hike, mountain-bike ride, or snowmobiling trip.

Figure 6.19
The Terrain layer is especially useful for hikers and climbers, because it shows elevations.

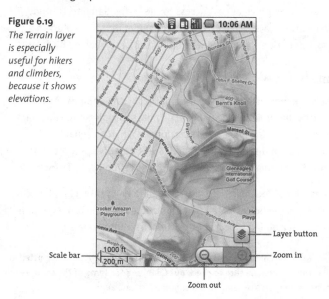

Layer button
Scale bar
Zoom in
Zoom out

Popular Categories

The Popular Categories option displays a list of popular search categories (such as restaurants, shopping, and lodging) when you conduct a search. Instead of having to type your search term, you can choose it from a list of categories instead. I'm not a big fan of this feature and keep it turned off, but don't let me bias you! Be sure to try it for yourself.

 I prefer to search via voice or standard text, because those methods involve fewer screen touches.

Layer button

The Layer button provides easy access to the Traffic, Satellite, Latitude, and Transit Lines layers (refer to Figure 6.5 earlier in this chapter). In my opinion, this option should be taken out of Labs and enabled by default.

Compass arrow

Arguably the most useful Labs feature of the lot, the Compass Arrow option uses the Droid's built-in digital compass to indicate the direction in which you're facing while you're stationary. When you enable this option, instead of displaying a dot on a map, Google Maps represents your location as an arrow that points in the direction you're facing.

That was a lot of technology to digest. In Chapter 7, I take a bit of a breather from the heavy technical jargon and have some fun reviewing the more entertaining aspects of the Droid: its multimedia apps.

 Maps has almost limitless applications over and beyond those listed in this chapter. Be sure to check out Chapter 8 for some of the creative ways that developers are using GPS technology in new apps.

The Best Part: Price

The best part about all this wonderful map technology is its price. It's *completely free*, in that it's included in the cost of your Droid and monthly data plan. I can't emphasize enough how important this is. Think about all the recurring monthly bills that you pay now: Internet access, mobile-phone plan, Starbucks card, and so on. They add up. The last thing you probably need is another monthly payment (or, even worse, another deduction from your checking account).

Although traditional GPS receivers freely use the circling government satellites to plot your location and help you navigate, many companies charge extra for add-on features such as traffic, weather, and sports scores. Also, don't forget the annual fees that some GPS providers charge for upgrading the maps on your GPS device, which can run about $50 per year. And don't get me started on how long it takes to load updated maps onto a GPS receiver.

With the Droid, all these features are included in your plan at no additional cost. This fact alone must be creating problems for GPS manufacturers; it's sure to cost them customers as people migrate to phone-based navigation, especially because the Droid's free service is feature-rich and doesn't require a dedicated GPS device.

7

Fun with Media

The past several chapters are rather utilitarian, focusing on tools like email, messaging, and contacts. Now it's time to let your hair down a little. In this chapter, I run down all the multimedia options that are available on the Droid, including photos, music, and movies. Let's have some fun, shall we?

note Numerous third-party applications that play (and record) multimedia are available from the Android Market. This chapter focuses on the applications that are preinstalled on the Droid; I cover third-party applications and the Android Market in Chapter 8.

Camera

A very useful feature of most modern smartphones is the built-in camera. It's incredibly convenient to be able to whip out your phone and snap a photo on demand. Because you always have your phone with you (at least, I do), it's easy to take a quick photo of the kids playing at the park—and the Internet access makes the Droid's camera even more powerful. Instead of just storing the photos for a rainy day, you can easily fire off an email to Nanny and attach the park photos. My wife and I find sending cameraphone photos by MMS to be especially useful for getting the other person's opinion on an appliance or piece of furniture. (See Chapter 5 for more about MMS.)

Traditionally, though, smartphones have a bad reputation for the image quality that their tiny cameras produce; many of these cameraphones are stuck at 2 megapixels. But the Droid is no slouch. It packs an impressive 5-megapixel autofocus camera with a dual-LED flash. It also boasts some pretty impressive specifications, including an image-capture area of 2592 x 1936 pixels for photos and a video-capture area of 720 x 380 pixels. And if all that weren't enough, the Droid's camera has image stabilization; white-balance control; geotagging; color effects; and built-in scene settings for things like sunset, snow, and beach. Holy Ansel Adams!

Taking photos

Taking photos with your Droid's camera is definitely an art, and getting it right takes a little practice. If you're patient and have a steady hand, however, the output from the Droid's camera can be quite impressive.

To take a photo on the Droid, follow these steps:

1. Launch the Camera app by pressing and holding the gold Camera key on the right side of the device or by touching the Camera icon in the application drawer.

2. Make sure that the slider is set to the Photo icon (**Figure 7.1**).

Thumbnail image

Video icon

Slider

Photo icon

Shutter-release button

Viewfinder

Figure 7.1 *The Camera app is mostly a giant viewfinder with an onscreen shutter-release button.*

3. Frame your subject with the viewfinder.

   You can hold the Droid horizontally or vertically.

4. Press halfway down on the Camera key to focus; then press all the way down to take the photo.

   Alternatively, you can touch the shutter-release button in the bottom-right corner of the screen (refer to Figure 7.1).

> **tip** Try to keep your Droid as still as possible when taking photos. A slight lag occurs between the time when you press the Camera key or shutter-release button and the time when the Droid actually captures the photo, making it difficult to photograph kids, pets and other fast-moving objects. For best results, try to keep your hands—and your subjects—still for a full second after you press the key or touch the button.

Pictures taken with the Droid's camera are automatically saved to the Gallery application, which I cover later in this chapter.

Reviewing photos

To review your photos instantly, touch the thumbnail image in the top-right corner of the screen (when the camera is held horizontally; refer to Figure 7.1 earlier in this chapter). When you touch the thumbnail, the image viewer opens, displaying the most recent photo taken and a row of menu buttons down the right edge of the screen (**Figure 7.2**).

Figure 7.2
Several options are available when you're reviewing an image.

These buttons are

- **Delete.** Touch this button to trash photos that are blurry or poorly composed.

- **Share.** The Share button allows you to send a photo immediately via email, Gmail, or the Messaging app or to Google's online photo service, Picasa (http://picasa.google.com).

> **tip** The list you see when you touch the Share button depends on what apps you have installed. Facebook and Twitter options, for example, appear in the list if you have the corresponding apps installed. (I cover third-party applications in Chapter 8.)

- **Set As.** After shooting, you can touch the Set As button to use the photo as a contact icon (which will be displayed when that person calls you on the phone; see Chapter 4) or as wallpaper for your Droid's home screen.

- **Done.** Touching Done closes the image viewer and returns you to the Camera app.

Configuring photo settings

While you're using the camera, you can press the Menu button and then touch Settings to access the Camera Settings screen (**Figure 7.3**). When you do, you get five options:

Figure 7.3
The Droid has more camera settings than some point-and-shoot cameras do.

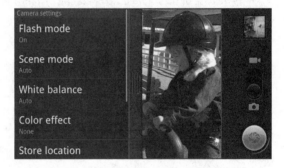

- **Flash Mode.** This option allows you to choose among Auto (the default), On, and Off.

- **Scene Mode.** One of my favorite Droid camera features, Scene Mode allows you to choose a setting that optimizes the camera for the type of photo you're taking. Your options are Auto (the default), Action, Portrait, Landscape, Night, Night Portrait, Theater, Beach, Snow, Sunset, and Steady Photo.

- **White Balance.** You have several white-balance choices, according to the lighting on your subject: Auto (the default), Incandescent, Daylight, Fluorescent, and Cloudy.

- **Color Effect.** Touching this option lets you apply one of several color effects to your photos, including Mono; Sepia; Negative, Solarize; and Red, Blue, and Green tints. The default setting is Auto, which applies none of these effects.

- **Store Location.** This option uses the Droid's Global Positioning System (GPS) chip to record your location in the photo data—a process called *geotagging*. This feature is turned off by default to save battery power.

Shooting video

With the release of the Android 2.0 operating system, the Droid's Camera app gained the ability to shoot DVD-quality video: 720- x 480-pixel video at 24 frames per second (fps). It also captures AAC audio in the process, so you won't be stuck with silent movies.

You don't want to toss your high-definition handycam just yet; the Droid's size limits the space available for the video sensor and associated electronics, so it's important to have realistic expectations. On the other hand, the Droid is a very capable camcorder and one of the most "pocket-able" video cameras around.

To shoot a video on the Droid, follow these steps:

1. Launch the Camera app by pressing and holding the gold Camera key on the right side of the device or by touching the Camera icon in the application drawer.

2. Set the slider to the Video icon (refer to Figure 7.1 earlier in this chapter).

3. Frame your subject, using the onscreen viewfinder.

4. Press the Droid's Camera key or touch the red button in the bottom-right corner of the screen to start and stop recording.

tip Numerous third-party applications extend the camera's functionality well beyond photos and movies. Some apps, for example, allow the camera to scan a product bar code and return comparison prices from the Internet. Read about some of the best Android applications in Chapter 8.

Gallery

The Camera app captures photos and video, and its companion app, Gallery, manages them. Launch Gallery by touching its icon in the application drawer. When you do, the image browser opens (**Figure 7.4**), displaying several thumbnail images that represent all of your various camera media, including any photos that you transferred to your Droid's microSD card.

Figure 7.4
The Gallery app's image browser.

Touch one of these images to reveal a thumbnail gallery of up to 15 photos at a time (**Figure 7.5**, on the next page). Flick your finger up and down the screen to scroll to the other photos in your library.

Figure 7.5
Thumbnail view allows you to view and scroll through your photos and videos quickly.

Viewing photos

To see a photo in full-screen mode, just touch its thumbnail in the image browser. When you're in full-screen mode, touching anywhere on the screen gives you several image options (**Figure 7.6**), including forward and backward arrows and the same Zoom In (+) and Zoom Out (–) icons that the Web browser uses (see Chapter 5).

Figure 7.6
Several options are available while you're viewing an image.

Touch the right arrow to advance to the next image or the left arrow to go back to the preceding image. The zoom icons allow you to zoom into and out of an image. Along the top of the screen are icons for the Set As, Share, and Delete options; these options function as I describe in the "Reviewing photos" section earlier in this chapter.

Setting photo options

After you've built up a library of photos (if you're like me, this won't take long), you can really have some fun with them. It's not much fun to keep all your photos bottled up in your Droid, so why not share them with friends in the moment? You don't need to wait to get home from a trip to share your photos; send a photo of yourself at the beach *from* the beach.

When you're in full-screen image mode, press the Menu button to reveal a list of choices (**Figure 7.7**):

Figure 7.7
Several menu options are available while you're viewing an image.

- **Share.** The Share button allows you to send a photo immediately via email, Gmail, or the Messaging app or to Google's Picasa service (see "Reviewing photos" earlier in this chapter).

- **Rotate.** This option turns your photo left or right in 90-degree increments.

- **Delete.** Touch this button to banish the current photo to the trash.

- **Crop.** This option lets you trim an image down to the good part easily by dragging an onscreen bounding box with your finger.

- **Set As.** The Set As option allows you to set a photo as a contact icon or as your phone's wallpaper. This feature works just like the Set As option in the Camera application (see "Reviewing photos" earlier in this chapter).

But wait! I can almost hear you saying, "There's one more button in Figure 7.7!" You're correct. The last button in the Photos menu is the infamous More button, which reveals another menu that offers more options still (**Figure 7.8**).

Figure 7.8
Several additional image options are available when you touch the More button.

These options are

- **Details.** Shows the details of a photo, including its file name, size, and resolution; the camera's manufacturer and model; the white-balance setting; and the date when the photo was taken.

- **Show on Maps.** Uses the GPS data collected where and when you took the photo—if you selected that option, that is—to show that location in Google Maps. (For more on Maps, see Chapter 6.)

- **Slideshow.** Displays your photos as a slideshow, advancing the photos automatically with a dissolve effect between photos—great for the plane ride home.

- **Settings.** Opens the General Settings screen (**Figure 7.9**). This screen is quite extensive, including options for changing the display size and sort order of photos. You can also set an option to have the Droid ask you to confirm before deleting photos. More useful are the transition-effect and slideshow-interval options. (Unfortunately, your interval choices are limited to 2, 3, or 4 seconds.) Finally, you have the option to set slideshows to repeat and to shuffle the photos instead of playing them in the order in which they were taken.

Figure 7.9
*Touch Menu >
More > Settings
to bring up
the Gallery
application's
General Settings
screen.*

Music

Now that you're an expert at taking photos and videos with your Droid, it's time to relax with some music. In addition to being a capable phone and camera, the Droid makes a great jukebox.

Before you start jamming on your Droid, you need to transfer some music to it. All music on the Droid is stored on its microSD card, which goes in the expansion-card slot. The Music application won't run unless a microSD card is installed.

> **tip** Although the 16 GB card included with your Droid is quite capable and should last a while, it will eventually fill up. Luckily, additional 16 GB and 32 GB cards are relatively inexpensive.

Android's Music application supports the following audio file formats:

- AAC, AAC+, eAAC+ (.3gp, .mp4, .m4a)
- MP3 (.mp3)
- MIDI (.mid and others)
- Ogg Vorbis (.ogg)

Sorry, Windows Media fans—the Droid has no WMA support.

> **note** To see how to transfer music to your Droid, flip to "Transferring files" later in this chapter.

Playing music

When you launch the Music application by touching its icon in the application drawer, you see the main Music interface (**Figure 7.10**), which is neatly divided into four logical areas that narrow your music down to artists, albums, songs, and playlists.

Figure 7.10

The main screen of the Music app is divided into four simple areas.

If you can't find what you're looking for, press the Menu button and then touch Search (**Figure 7.11**). Alternatively, if you're not in the mood to think, touch Party Shuffle to play randomly selected tunes.

Figure 7.11

Press the Menu button to search or shuffle your music collection.

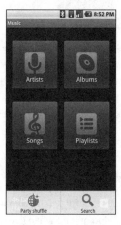

Artists view

Artists view (**Figure 7.12**) displays all the music on your memory card sorted by artist. Flick up and down to scroll. Touch any artist to drill down to all the songs by that artist, and touch a song to start playing it.

Figure 7.12

The Artists screen in the Music app. Touch the little arrow button next to an artist's name to display all the albums by that artist.

While a song is playing, you'll see its detail view (**Figure 7.13**), which provides some basic information about the song. Below the album artwork are Playlist, Shuffle, and Repeat buttons, followed by the artist, album, and song name. At the very bottom of the screen are the standard Play/Pause, Fast Forward, and Rewind buttons; the timeline; the time elapsed; and the total time.

Albums view

Albums view, as you've probably guessed, displays your music sorted by album (**Figure 7.14**). This view is helpful when you have a lot of complete albums, but it can get kind of long when you have a mishmosh of music or a bunch of music in one particular genre. Albums view displays the album artwork (assuming that you have it), album name, and artist for all the music that you have loaded on your memory card.

Figure 7.13
A song's detail view is displayed whenever that song is played.

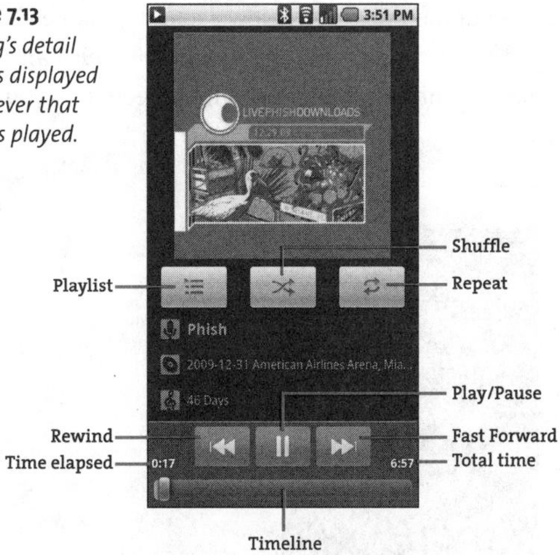

Shuffle

Playlist

Repeat

Play/Pause

Rewind

Fast Forward

Time elapsed

Total time

Timeline

Figure 7.14
The Music app's Albums view.

Songs view

Songs view (**Figure 7.15**) is also pretty self-explanatory, displaying
every song loaded on your memory card. Below each song name is the
artist, and to the right is the song's running time. Simply touch any
song to play it, or flick your finger up and down the screen until you find
something that you like.

Figure 7.15
*Songs view in the
Music app.*

> **tip** One of my favorite things to do in Songs view is flick-shuffle, which
> involves giving the song list a good flick and then randomly touching
> the screen to stop at a song. Think of this technique as being like spinning that
> big wheel in the Showcase Showdown on "The Price Is Right," except that you
> don't have to wait for the wheel to stop.

Playlists view

Finally, you can view your music by playlist (**Figure 7.16**) when you touch
the Playlist button in the main Music screen. The Droid supports .m3u
playlists, which it reads from the microSD card.

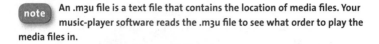

note An .m3u file is a text file that contains the location of media files. Your music-player software reads the .m3u file to see what order to play the media files in.

Figure 7.16
Playlists view in the Music app.

If you want to use playlists, create a Playlists folder inside the Music folder on your memory card, and copy your .m3u files to it. After you do, your playlists will show up whenever you touch the Playlists button.

Transferring files

Moving photos, videos, and music (and all other files, for that matter) between your Droid and a desktop computer is easy. Just follow these steps:

1. Connect your Droid to any PC or Mac with the included USB cable.

   When it's connected, your Droid will display a USB icon in the status bar.

2. Drag down from the status bar to reveal the notification window, and touch USB Connected.

3. Touch Mount.

   Your Droid's SD card will appear in My Computer (Windows) or on the Desktop (Mac).

4. Transfer the files via drag and drop or copy and paste.

5. Slide your finger down from the status bar to reveal the notifications window, and touch Turn off USB Storage.

6. Unplug the USB cable, and you're done!

tip Another way to transfer files to the Droid is to insert the microSD card into an SD card carrier and then insert the carrier into a card reader connected to your computer. At that point, you can copy the files to the card.

note You can keep tabs on how much space is available on your Droid's microSD card by touching Settings > SD Card & Phone Storage. Other options allow you to unmount and format your microSD card.

Buying and playing Amazon MP3 files

In addition to transferring music from your own library to the Droid, you can purchase music directly on the device, over the air (OTA). The Amazon MP3 app (**Figure 7.17**), which is preinstalled on the Droid, allows you to buy any of more than 10 million songs. Most best-selling tracks cost 99 cents, and albums start at $7.99 each. It's nice to have the option to download tracks directly to the device for those "gotta hear it" moments and for the times when your own playlists start sounding a little stale.

Figure 7.17
*The Amazon
MP3 application
allows you to buy
music over the air
directly to your
Droid.*

Amazon MP3 is pretty straightforward in design, featuring four main ways to browse its catalog: by top 100 albums, top 100 tracks, or genre and by searching. Although you can browse anonymously, you need an account to purchase music from the Amazon MP3 app. I recommend that you set up your account on a desktop computer (if you don't already have an Amazon.com account, that is).

If using your Droid is the only option, here's how to do it:

1. Visit Amazon.com in the Droid's Web browser (refer to Chapter 5).

2. Touch the Your Account link at the bottom of the page.

3. Touch the button labeled No, I Am a New Customer.

4. Follow the onscreen instructions to create a new account.

   During this process, you need to enter your preferred payment method by going to the Your Account section, scrolling down to the Payment section, and touching Add a Credit Card. You also need to check the box labeled Make This My Default 1-Click Credit Card so that you can download MP3s from the Amazon MP3 mobile store.

When you've done all that, you're ready to go. Just try to keep the impulse purchases in check. Set weekly or monthly spending limits, and try not to exceed them. Just try!

More Than Music

You can also use music and audio files from your computer as alarms, notifications, and ringtones on the Droid. Simply create folders named Alarms, Notifications, and Ringtones at the root level of the microSD card; then copy the appropriate files to the correct folders. The next time you set an alarm, notification, or ringtone, you'll see your music files as choices. Cool!

YouTube

As I mention in Chapter 1, Google acquired YouTube in 2006 for $1.65 billion, so if you bet that Google would include a YouTube player on the Droid, you'd be correct!

YouTube for Android is more than just a simple video player. In fact, it includes several features that are available on YouTube.com, including a huge catalog of keyword-searchable videos, and it allows you to browse videos in several ways (most popular, most viewed, top rated, most recent, and most discussed). Just flick your finger up and down across the screen to scroll through the videos. These lists are a great way to keep yourself entertained on a long trip without having to search for video (provided that you have an Internet connection).

When you touch the YouTube icon to launch the application (**Figure 7.18**), you see the most-viewed videos, followed by most-discussed and most-recent. Next to each thumbnail image are the video's name, description, rating, upload time, and number of views. You can also touch the circular *i* icon to reveal a wealth of additional information, such as comments and related videos.

Figure 7.18
*The main
YouTube
interface.*

note YouTube on Android is limited to videos encoded in H.264/MPEG-4. This means that only videos encoded in H.264 will play on the Droid; videos encoded in Adobe Flash are *not* supported.

Pressing the Menu button reveals five options:

- **Search.** Allows you to search for videos by entering example text (such as *Tenacious D*).

- **Upload.** Allows you to select a video from the Gallery app (refer to "Gallery" earlier in this chapter) or any third-party video application that you have installed.

- **My Account.** Allows you to log in to your account to view information about your videos.

- **Categories**. Displays a list of more than 50 categories of videos, including Music, People & Blogs, and Science & Technology.

- **Settings.** Allows you to clear your search history, filter videos by time, and read YouTube's terms-of-service agreement.

Watching a video is as simple as touching its thumbnail image. You'll have to rotate your Droid to landscape view to view YouTube videos, but that's OK, because you get more screen real estate that way. (I hope that you find this view comfortable, because landscape view is all that the Droid supports.) From there, you operate the onscreen buttons pretty much the same way that you did on the first VCR you bought 20 years ago. Play, fast-forward, and rewind, baby!

The YouTube app for Android 2.0 has many new features, the biggest one being the ability to log in to your account at YouTube.com (by touching Menu > My Account) so that you can play and view statistical information about videos that you previously uploaded. You can even manage your personal subscriptions in the My Account screen (**Figure 7.19**).

Because the Droid allows you to shoot DVD-quality video (as I discuss in "Shooting video" earlier in this chapter), you can upload your videos directly to YouTube from the phone. The Droid's ability to add effects such as solarization and tints to your videos will channel your inner Martin Scorsese before you know it.

The Droid's stunning screen (3.7 inches diagonally, 854 x 480 pixels, 16 million colors) is one of the best on any smartphone, which also makes it one of the best phones for playing videos. By default, YouTube videos are played in high quality on the Droid when you're using Wi-Fi (see Chapter 3). If you're out of Wi-Fi range, you can still watch videos in high definition by touching Menu > More > Watch in High Quality.

Figure 7.19

Logging in to your YouTube account allows you to upload videos and view information about your videos.

The controls of the YouTube app for Droid are much like those in the desktop version of YouTube, allowing you to search, share, rate, comment on, and view videos on the go.

note The YouTube widget (accessible by long-pressing the YouTube icon in the home screen and then touching Widgets) gives you easy access to recording and sharing capabilities right from your Droid's home screen.

So there you have it. Take some time to learn the lighter side of Android. It can be great to share your photos, unwind to some tunes, and get a quick laugh courtesy of a video on YouTube.

Now that I've covered most of the included applications on Android, it's time to cast a wider net. In Chapter 8, I give you an overview of the Android Market, where you can choose among thousands of applications to download and review some of the best ones available from this wonderful resource.

8

Android Market

The most powerful and fun application on the Droid is the Android Market. It's fun because it has so many types of applications available for the Droid. There's something for everyone.

Part of the strength of the Market is its catalog of more than 20,000 applications. Although that catalog isn't as deep as Apple's App Store, the Android Market is starting to challenge Apple's dominance in mobile-app distribution. Check out these Market milestones:

- March 2009: 2,300 applications available for download

- November 2009: 12,000

- December 2009: 20,000

It may have gotten off to a slow start, but the Market is a fast-growing treasure chest of goodies for owners of Droids, and it's getting better all the time as it matures into an enticing platform for developers of Android apps.

In this chapter, I show you how to use the Android Market and highlight some of the best applications that I've found.

note This chapter covers the version of Market that comes with Android 2.0. Earlier versions will look different and offer fewer features.

Navigating the Market

 The Market application comes preinstalled on all Android-powered phones. To launch it, simply touch the Market icon—the one with the friendly robot on a shopping bag.

Like most applications for Android, Market has a dead-simple interface. When you launch the app, you're greeted by a tidy, well-organized home screen that's optimized for the Droid's small display (**Figure 8.1**).

tip If you want to get started right away, just touch an app's icon and then install it. If you don't see something of interest right away, try a few searches; you may be pleasantly surprised.

The home screen gives you several ways to navigate the Android Market:

- **Search.** In the top-right corner of the screen is a magnifying-glass icon. To use it, simply touch the icon and type a few keywords in the resulting search field. A search for *golf* in February 2010 produced 71 results, including applications for keeping score and tracking your exact position on the course via satellite—not to mention golf jokes. Search for the names of your hobbies, and you'll probably find some interesting selections.

Figure 8.1
*The Android
Market's home
screen.*

- **Category buttons.** Across the top of the main Market screen is a navigation bar containing three buttons:

    - **Apps.** Touching the Apps button reveals a catch-all list of categories, such as Communication, Finance, and Reference. Touch a category to see a list of all the applications in that category, sortable by paid, free, and newest.

    - **Games.** This area of the Market is for the gamer in you. Touch the Games button to reveal numerous categories, from Action and Arcade to Cards and Casino.

    - **Verizon.** Because the Motorola Droid is exclusive to Verizon Wireless, the carrier gets its own button in the Market. Touching the Verizon button displays a page of apps designed or distributed by that carrier, including MyVerizon, Visual Voice Mail, and Verizon FiOS Mobile.

note   Droid Eris owners won't have the Verizon button.

- **Top bar.** Directly below the navigation bar is the top bar, which contains big, colorful icons for apps in a given category. This bar displays only three icons at a time, rotating them every 5 seconds or so. Because all the icons in the top bar represent a category (in Figure 8.1, the category is Casual), touching any of those icons takes you to a page of all the apps in that category, as opposed to a page for that individual app.

- **Featured section.** Below the animated top bar is a list of featured applications. Next to each icon, you see the app's name, the developer's name, the price, and the user rating. Slide your finger up and down the screen to scroll through the list. Touching any of the featured icons takes you to the detail-view page for that application.

 Google constantly updates the Featured section of the Market, so it's a good idea to check periodically to see what's new.

An app's detail-view page (**Figure 8.2**) displays a wealth of information. Scroll down to find screen shots and user reviews (which Google refers to as *comments*) of the app, links to more apps by the developer, and the application's Web site.

Figure 8.2
A detail-view page for a Market application.

If you haven't installed the application, you'll see a large Install (if it's free) or Buy (if it's paid) button at the bottom of the screen. If you already have the app installed, you'll see Open and Uninstall buttons, which do just what their names suggest.

Buying an App

note You need to have a Google Checkout account to buy apps from the Android Market. If you don't have an account, you can set one up at www.google.com/checkout.

Purchasing an app in the Android Market is actually quite easy. Here's all you have to do:

1. Launch the Market (if it isn't already running) by touching its icon.

2. Navigate to the app you want to buy, following the directions in the preceding section.

3. Touch the app's icon to open its detail-view page (refer to Figure 8.2).

4. Touch the Buy button at the bottom of the page.

5. Touch first OK and then Buy Now in the checkout screen.

   The app downloads to your Droid.

Read the Fine Print Before Buying

When you've found an application that you want to purchase, consider a few things before touching the Buy button:

- **Reinstallations.** Android Market allows you to reinstall purchased apps an unlimited number of times at no charge. This feature comes in handy when you get a new phone (provided that it runs Android, that is) or when a factory reset is necessary.

- **Returns.** The Market accepts returns within 24 hours of purchase (not download). The clock starts ticking the moment you purchase an app, not whenever you get around to installing it, so you should try to use an app immediately after installing it. You may return a given application only one time; if you purchase the same application again later, you can't return it a second time.

tip Market returns are handled directly in each application. Just touch the icon for the app in question and then touch Uninstall & Refund. If the refund option isn't there, your 24-hour return window has passed.

- **Billing disputes.** Google is not responsible for billing disputes arising from Android Market purchases. All billing issues should be directed to the developer in question, the payment processor, or your credit-card company, as appropriate.

Updating Your Purchases

Developers frequently release updates to their apps to add features and fix bugs. When an update is available for an Android Market application that you've already downloaded, your Droid displays a notification icon in the status bar (**Figure 8.3**). Swipe your finger from the status bar down to reveal the details; then touch Updates Available and follow the prompts to install the updates.

Figure 8.3
A status-bar icon notifies you when updates are available for apps you've downloaded from the Android Market.

Market notification icon

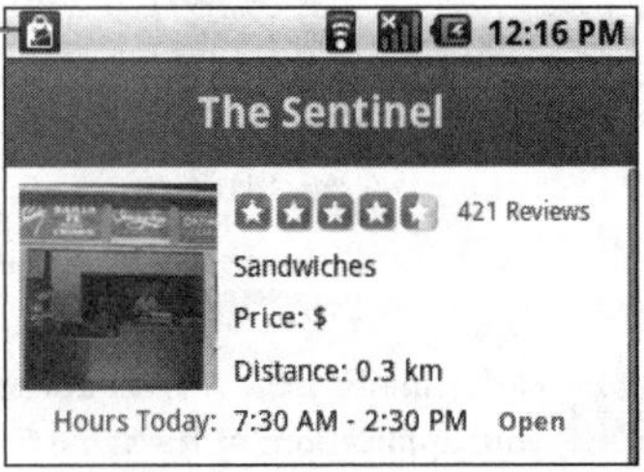

The Sentinel

421 Reviews
Sandwiches
Price: $
Distance: 0.3 km
Hours Today: 7:30 AM - 2:30 PM   Open

12:16 PM

You can easily check to see whether any of the apps that you've downloaded are out of date by launching Market and touching Menu > Downloads. The Droid takes you to the Downloads screen (**Figure 8.4**, on the next page), which lists all the applications that you've downloaded to date. Applications that have pending updates are displayed at the top of the list, with the text *Update available* next to them in orange. To install an update, just touch the app; then touch Update, followed by OK. Updates are downloaded in the background, allowing you to do other things on your Droid while they download.

Figure 8.4
The Downloads screen puts apps that have pending updates at the top of the list.

note Unfortunately, the Market doesn't give you an easy way to update all your applications at the same time. Perhaps we'll see this feature added in a future update of the Market application.

The rest of the apps in the Downloads list are displayed in reverse chronological order, with your most recent downloads listed first.

Checking out Some Special Apps

Following are some of the most interesting applications that I've discovered in my travels around the Android Market, listed in no particular order. Some are free, and some are paid (as noted); all of them are unique. Feel free to try them out.

Google Voice

Price: Free

Developer: Google (www.google.com/mobile/voice)

Google Voice (**Figure 8.5**) allows you to make calls through Google and bypass the telecom carriers entirely. Instead of using the native Phone application to make telephone calls, you make them with Google Voice for Mobile instead.

This amazing service gives you a free Google telephone number that rings all your phones when someone calls it. It also allows you to make calls and send free text messages from this free number. The best part is that when someone leaves you a voice-mail message in your Google Voice inbox, it's automatically transcribed and can be sent to you as an email or SMS text message. Conference calling and low-priced international calling round out a feature set that's irresistible.

Figure 8.5
The Google Voice inbox.

When Google Voice allows users to port home phone numbers to it, I'll be the first in line. The service promises to let users divorce their phone carriers once and for all.

ShopSavvy

Price: Free

Developer: Big in Japan, Inc. (www.biggu.com/apps/shopsavvy-android)

ShopSavvy (**Figure 8.6**) turns your Droid into a portable comparison-shopping research assistant. It uses the camera in your phone to scan the bar code on any product and then finds the best prices on the Internet and at nearby local stores. Just fire it up, point your Droid's camera at virtually any bar code, and wait for the beep. ShopSavvy displays a list of results for that item, including prices.

Figure 8.6
ShopSavvy compares prices over the Internet for anything with a bar code.

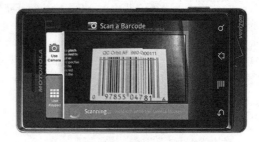

note Shop Savvy recently added support for scanning those funky square QR codes, too.

WeatherBug Elite

Price: $1.99

Developer: WeatherBug (www.weatherbug.com)

Although several free weather apps are available for the Droid, WeatherBug is my favorite weather app for Android. It lets you view current conditions, forecasts, National Weather Service (NWS) alerts, radar, maps, camera views, and video. It also offers location-based preferences and an excellent widget for your Droid's home screen.

The Elite version (**Figure 8.7**) includes enhanced contour weather maps showing lightning strikes, humidity, pressure, and wind speed; radar animation; and an additional home-screen widget that displays an extended three-day forecast. My favorite feature is the locations summary page, which displays weather conditions for all of your saved locations.

Figure 8.7
WeatherBug Elite is the best weather app for Droid—well worth the $2.

My Tracks

Price: Free

Developer: Google (http://mytracks.appspot.com)

I bet that My Tracks (**Figure 8.8**) was developed by a team at Google that's into outdoor sports, because this app allows your Droid to record live GPS and output statistics about your run, hike, or bike ride over a given period, including your location, speed, distance, and elevation. You can upload all this data to Google Spreadsheets and Google Maps, and if you're competitive, you can even share your results with a friend. After you've captured several sets of data from your daily run or bike ride, you can track your progress.

Figure 8.8

My Tracks can use your GPS coordinates to record your tracks.

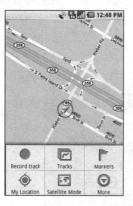

To use My Tracks, make sure that GPS is turned on (touch Settings > Location & Security > Use GPS Satellites), launch the app, and touch Menu > Record Track. You'll see yourself represented as a small triangle on a Google map. Go do your thing, and when you're finished, touch Stop.

Whether you're a casual outdoors type or a diehard triathlete, you'll definitely get a kick out of My Tracks.

Twidroid Pro

Price: $4.99

Developer: Zimmermann & Marban (www.twidroid.com)

Twitter is a love-it-or-hate-it type of thing, and if you love it, I've got a Twitter client for you: Twidroid Pro (**Figure 8.9**). It's the de facto standard Twitter client for Android and seems perfectly at home on the Droid. A free version is available, but the Pro version is worth the five bucks, which gets you support for multiple accounts, video posting, and themes.

Figure 8.9
Twidroid Pro is one of the most full-featured Twitter clients on the market.

If that weren't enough, Twidroid Pro offers a laundry list of other excellent features, such as native bit.ly support, an integrated buzz viewer (trends), and additional support for URL shorteners and photo-posting services.

Locale

Price: $9.99

Developer: two forty four a.m. (www.twofortyfouram.com)

Locale (**Figure 8.10**) turns location management into an art form. This app dynamically manages all of your Droid's settings, based on conditions such as location and time. You can use it to set up a condition that turns off 3G and switches to your home Wi-Fi network as soon as the phone is in range. You can even set it up so that designated VIP callers always ring through, no matter how you've set the phone's ringer volume.

Figure 8.10
Locale allows you to set rules for things such as when and how your Droid rings.

Video Player

Price: Free

Developer: Jeff Hamilton, Google (www.google.com)

Although the Droid's Gallery app (which I cover in Chapter 7) scans the entire microSD card for media and will play video files, it's not a full-fledged video player. Luckily, third-party developers are addressing that omission.

For playing videos, I recommend Jeff Hamilton's basic Video Player (**Figure 8.11**). It plays video files from the SD card and supports numerous formats, including MPEG4 or 3GPP with H.264 or H.263 and MP3, AAC, and AMR audio. Videos need to be 480 x 352 pixels or smaller to play back properly.

tip   If this app doesn't have enough horsepower for you, several other video player apps are available in the Market, including aPlayer, Act 1, and Cinema.

Figure 8.11
Video Player is a free basic video player for the Droid.

MyBackup Pro

Price: $4.99

Developer: RerWare (www.rerware.com/MyBackup)

MyBackup Pro (**Figure 8.12**) isn't the sexiest app in the Android Market, but if your Droid gets lost or damaged, you'll wish that you used it. It can restore data and applications easily on the same phone or a new one.

Figure 8.12
MyBackup Pro can back up all your important information to the cloud in case you ever lose or change phones.

MyBackup Pro can back up your Droid's data to an SD card or to RerWare's secure online servers. It can also back up your installation files so that you don't have to download all your applications again if you wipe or change phones. The best part is that you can schedule it to back up your phone at a set interval. (Let's face it—nobody *always* remembers to back up.)

tip I highly recommend that you store your backups on RerWare's servers in addition to storing them on your microSD card. If you lose your phone, you're going to lose the microSD card that's inside it, along with your data. All data that you store online, however, is kept private and secure.

ASTRO File Manager

Price: Free

Developer: Metago (www.metago.net/astro/fm)

ASTRO File Manager (**Figure 8.13**) gives you tools to manage all the files on your Droid. It won't be of much use to a novice user, but it's a tinkerer's dream come true. With this app, you can copy, move, delete, and rename files on your SD card. You can even work with multiple files and directories at the same time. The application runs in the background, so your actions will be completed even if you receive a phone call during the process.

ASTRO allows you to send files as attachments; view thumbnails and images; and even browse and create compressed files, including .zip and .tar. You can also use it to back up applications and manage running applications. It's literally a Swiss-army-knife app for Android.

Figure 8.13
ASTRO is the best file manager for Android, hands down.

Advanced Task Manager

Price: 99 cents

Developer: Arron La (www.arronla.com)

Background apps are among the defining features of the Android operating system. It's handy to listen to a streaming Internet radio station while you're replying to email, for example. The problem is that apps running in the background consume precious battery life and other system resources. If you don't need to have them running, you'd be better off killing them.

Advanced Task Manager (**Figure 8.14**) is a super-handy app that lets you view, edit, and end any of the applications (processes) that are running on your Droid. You can also view the memory footprint of each app and instantly switch to any running app. On your schedule, the application also frees all your memory except for the apps you specify, and it comes with a widget too.

Figure 8.14
Advanced Task Manager allows you to kill unnecessary processes, saving battery life.

Amazon.com

Price: Free

Developer: Amazon (www.amazon.com/gp/anywhere/sms/android)

Amazon.com is America's largest retailer and purveyor of everything from books and music to electronics and computers. In addition to offering a killer selection of goods with fast shipping, Amazon makes it easy to buy. User-contributed reviews help make the decision-making process a little easier.

Another way that Amazon continues to be successful is making compelling apps for mobile phones. The Amazon app for Android (**Figure 8.15**) allows you to shop from your phone just as easily as you can from your computer.

Figure 8.15
Amazon.com is a must-have app if you shop Amazon a lot.

The app allows you to shop in more than 40 categories of merchandise offered by Amazon and its partner merchants. You can access your account, cart, wish lists, and all your various payment and shipment settings.

The best feature of the Amazon Android app (say *that* three times fast) is searching by bar code or photo. To use this feature—which is called Amazon Remembers—touch the link below the search bar and then snap a photo or bar code with the Droid's camera. The image is analyzed by real humans at Amazon, and you'll get a reply that includes purchasing options.

Google Goggles

Price: Free

Developer: Google (www.google.com/mobile/goggles)

This app is still in Google's labs, which means that it isn't final, but I have no reservations about recommending Goggles (**Figure 8.16**). This free app allows you to search the Web with your Droid's camera. If you don't want to type or speak your search query, you can search a third way: by photo.

Figure 8.16
Goggles allows you to search with your Droid's camera.

With Goggles, you can take photos of bar codes and products like books and DVDs, just as you can with Amazon's app (see the preceding section). What makes Google's app different, however, is that it's not limited to one store. Also, you can take photos of things like business cards, signs, artwork, and landmarks and submit them for searching. Submitting a photo of a real-estate yard sign, for example, returns information about the home's online listing.

The killer—and surprisingly underhyped—feature of Goggles is its augmented-reality mode. Simply point the camera at a store, and you'll see links to Google information about it (and surrounding businesses) onscreen, overlaid on the live video feed.

Google Sky Map

Price: Free

Developer: Google (www.google.com/sky/skymap.html)

Google Sky Map (**Figure 8.17**) is one of my favorite Android apps because it's fun and educational at the same time. Its slogan, "The universe in your pocket," pretty much sums it up.

Figure 8.17
Google Sky Map turns your Droid into a pocket telescope, annotated by Google.

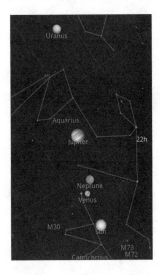

Like a few of my other favorite apps (Layar, Wikitude, and Goggles), Google Sky Map uses a new technology called augmented reality, which displays information from the Web in an overlay on your camera's live video feed. The technology is in its infancy, but it's already breathtaking and has a ton of potential.

With Google Sky Map, you just point your Droid at the night sky and browse planets, stars, and constellations on the screen of your phone. As you pan across the sky, Google Sky Map updates in real time, allowing you to match stars with their names. It's very well done and worth the download.

Pandora

Price: Free

Developer: Pandora (www.pandora.com/android)

Pandora is my favorite music service, bar none. Its Droid app (**Figure 8.18**) allows you to stream music directly to your phone simply by entering an artist name or a few keywords. The service searches the Music Genome Project—a huge catalog of music categorized by more than 400 musical attributes.

Figure 8.18
Pandora streams free music directly to your Droid.

It's simple to set up a station based on an artist that you like. I can't live without my Dub Reggae, Deep House, and Lounge radio stations, for example. Try setting up a station for Frank Sinatra for dinner music and even one for modern jazz, if that floats your boat.

Pandora is a requirement on my desktop computer (I write all my books with Pandora on in the background), and it's also a requirement on my phones.

Facebook

Price: Free

Developer: Facebook (www.facebook.com/apps/application.
php?id=74769995908)

Facebook, like Twitter, is a love-it-or-hate-it kind of thing. Some people
get through life without ever using Facebook, while others spend a good
portion of theirs using the popular social-networking site. Whether you're
a hardcore daily user or a casual user who checks in only periodically, there
are lots of reasons to have the Facebook app installed on your Droid.

Facebook for Android (**Figure 8.19**) makes it easy to stay connected with
your online friends. It allows you to share status updates, read your news-
feeds, and peruse your friends' walls and user information. You can also
share photos easily and look up your friends' phone numbers right from
the home screen.

Figure 8.19
*Facebook for
Android is
essential for
regular users
of the social-
networking site.*

DoggCatcher

Price: $10

Developer: SnoggDoggler (www.snoggdoggler.com)

DoggCatcher (**Figure 8.20**) is the premiere podcast client (sometimes called a *podcatcher*) for Android. With it, you can download and stream any of the millions of podcasts that are available on the Internet directly to your Droid.

Figure 8.20
DoggCatcher allows you to listen to podcasts on your Droid.

The app comes with a preset group of podcasts to get you started. You can also browse the top 100 feeds, search for a podcast, or receive podcast recommendations based on your settings.

The cool part is that DoggCatcher streams audio podcasts over both Wi-Fi and 3G connections. It even remembers the play position of each podcast, so if your listening session gets interrupted, you can instantly pick up where you left off.

FindMyPhone

Price: $1

Developer: Mango Bird (http://sites.google.com/site/findmyphone1)

FindMyPhone (**Figure 8.21**) is an ingenious app that makes it easier to find your phone when you lose it. I don't know about you, but I lose my phone at least once a day, and this app is a great way to locate a phone that's gone missing.

Figure 8.21
FindMyPhone locates your lost Droid.

It works like this: Download and install FindMyPhone on your Droid, and when you inevitably lose it, just send it a text message (SMS). Your Droid will reply with its current location. If the location doesn't help, you can also make your phone ring loudly for several minutes—a convenient feature when you lose your phone inside your home.

FlightTrack Pro

Price: $9.99

Developer: Mobiata LLC (www.mobiata.com/android-apps)

FlightTrack Pro (**Figure 8.22**) is the best app in its class because it has a super-clean interface and provides real-time flight itinerary updates at a glance. Its combination of usability and features is unmatched in the Android Market.

Figure 8.22

FlightTrack Pro is the best flight-tracking app for Android.

You can enter your flight info directly into FlightTrack Pro, but I recommend that you set up a free account at TripIt.com instead. Then just forward your flight-confirmation emails to plans@tripit.com, and all your flight information automatically appears on your Droid in FlightTrack.

TripIt saves a ton of time that you'd otherwise spend manually entering flight information in your phone, which alone is worth the price of admission.

The app gives you all the tracking features you'd expect, including up-to-date data on flight cancellations, delays, and gate changes. Tapping any segment displays your full TripIt itinerary in the browser. FlightTrack Pro will even alert you to flight-status updates via push notifications even when the app isn't open.

Finally, when you're traveling, the cool home-screen widget is worth its weight in gold.

Yelp

Price: Free

Developer: Yelp (www.yelp.com)

Yelp (**Figure 8.23**) provides user-generated reviews of all kinds of businesses, but it's predominantly known for its reviews of eateries. If you're out of town and looking for a good place to nosh, Yelp has what you're looking for.

Figure 8.23

Yelp is a great way to find restaurant reviews when you're out of town.

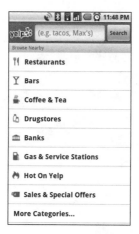

Yelp reportedly enjoys more than 25 million visits each month to its Web site, which consistently ranks among the top 100 U.S. Web sites.

To use it, launch the app and then choose one of the numerous categories below Browse Nearby. If you select Restaurants, you'll get a list of all the Yelp-reviewed restaurants near your current location, thanks to the Droid's handy GPS chip. Each listing includes the restaurant's name, location, cuisine, price, and distance, as well as reviews. Dig into the reviews, and you'll have more information than you could ever imagine about just about any restaurant in the United States. Good stuff!

Layar

Price: Free

Developer: Layar (www.layar.com)

Layar (**Figure 8.24**) bills itself as a "mobile augmented-reality browser." As you can see from some of my other app selections, augmented reality is a hotbed of technology innovation.

Figure 8.24
Layar provides a breathtaking way to navigate a new place.

Layar displays real-time information—such as houses for sale, shops, and tourist and concert information—over the live video coming from your Droid's camera.

9

Resources

I hope that this *Pocket Guide* helped you get up and running on your Droid quickly. If you'd like to do further research any of the topics I covered, the Internet has a wealth of additional information that you can peruse on your own schedule. In this chapter, I list several useful Web sites that can further your knowledge of all things Droid.

Google Links

Because Google is so tightly integrated with the Droid, you'll find your-self using a lot of its products online in a desktop Web browser. Here are a few Web sites that you'll want to use to get the most out of your Droid:

www.google.com/calendar

www.google.com/contacts

www.google.com/latitude

www.google.com/mail

www.google.com/maps

www.youtube.com

Mobile apps

To find out more about Google's mobile apps, like the ones that ship on the Droid, just add the word *mobile* to the URL, as follows:

www.google.com/mobile/goggles

www.google.com/mobile/mail

www.google.com/mobile/maps

www.google.com/mobile/navigation

www.google.com/mobile/voice

www.google.com/mobile/youtube

 note Many Google mobile sites have excellent instructional videos showing the apps in action.

Google blogs

Google blogs are probably the best sources of information about the company's products. Extremely talented Google engineers and product managers wax poetic in their blogs about the company's latest products, and information breaks there first. Here are a few good blogs to follow:

http://googleblog.blogspot.com

http://google-latlong.blogspot.com

http://googlemobile.blogspot.com

If you *really* have a lot of time on your hands, Google lists almost 100 blogs in its blog directory, organized by products, ads, developers, region, and Google-wide:

www.google.com/press/blogs/directory.html

Android Developer Challenge (ADC)

Each year, Google holds the Android Developer Challenge (ADC), giving prizes for the best applications for the Android operating system. Google awards a $100,000 top prize, $50,000 second prize, and $25,000 third prize in each of ten categories, including Lifestyle, Productivity, and Games. The stakes are high, and winning apps get a big spike in sales after the winners are announced. Find out about the ADC here:

http://code.google.com/android/adc/gallery_winners.html

tip **Another consistently good Web site for app ideas is Android Network Awards Winners (www.androidguys.com/2009/08/18/presenting-the-android-network-awards-winners).**

YouTube

Because Google owns YouTube, it's logical that the ubiquitous video player would end up on the Droid. In the very definition of a symbiotic relationship, Google also posts all of its Android tutorial videos on YouTube, and they're fantastic resources. Check out these sites:

www.youtube.com/androidtips

www.youtube.com/user/Google

Phone links

The Droid wouldn't be the Droid without all the players. Various Web sites, including these, provide lots of information and technical support:

http://phones.verizonwireless.com/motorola/droid

http://www.htc.com/us/products/droid-eris-verizon

http://www.motorola.com/Consumers/US-EN/Consumer-Product-and-Services/Mobile-Phones/ci.Motorola-DROID-US-EN.alt

https://supportforums.motorola.com

Software updates

It's best to keep your Android software up to date. Here's where to find the latest software for the Droid:

http://support.vzw.com/information/droid_eris_upgrade.html

http://support.vzw.com/information/droid_upgrade.html

Third-Party Links

In addition to all the Web sites maintained by Google and its manufacturing and carrier partners, you can find hundreds more that are painstakingly updated by members of the Android community, including these:

www.androidcentral.com

www.androidguys.com

www.androidtapp.com

www.googleandblog.com

www.helloandroid.com

www.intomobile.com/category/platforms/android

www.tmonews.com/category/android

@Twitter

Many Android bloggers and developers maintain Twitter accounts. Here are some of the accounts whose tweets you need to follow:

http://twitter.com/androidcentral

http://twitter.com/androidguys

http://twitter.com/droidbuzz

http://twitter.com/htc

http://twitter.com/verizonwireless

That's a Wrap

So there you have it, folks! You've had a good look at everything from unboxing your Droid to configuring it to installing applications on it.

I hope that you enjoyed reading this book as much as I enjoyed writing it. More important, I hope that it helps you squeeze every little bit of potential out of the Droid.

Index